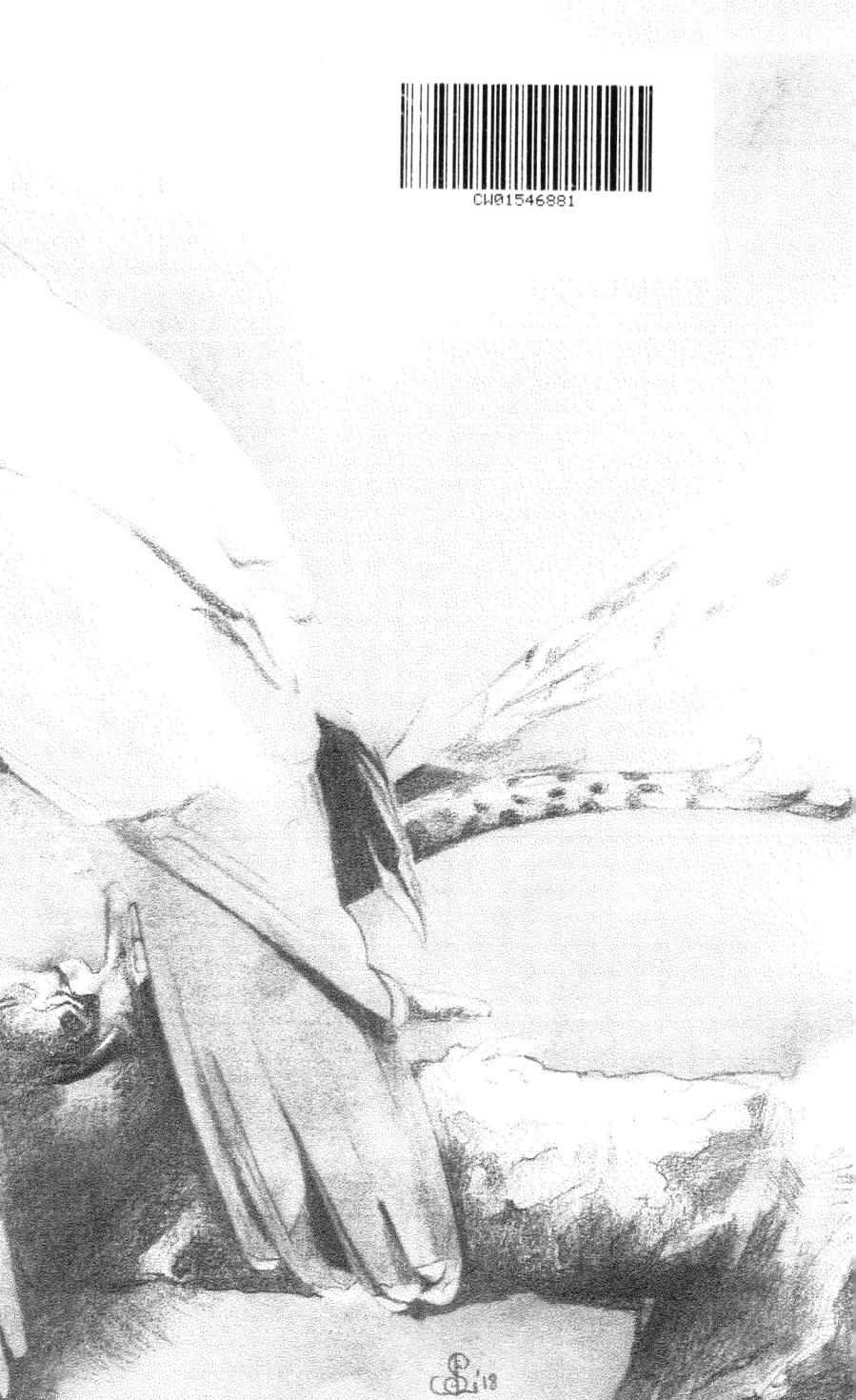

form
UNVEILING THE SUN

Unveiling the Sun

A MAYO JOURNAL

Seán Lysaght

SEÁN LYSAGHT

With drawings by Yvonne McDermott

Stonechat Editions

First published in 2025
by
Stonechat Editions
Fahy
Westport
County Mayo
Ireland
F28 YD65

Text copyright © Seán Lysaght
Illustrations copyright © Yvonne McDermott
Endpapers image copyright © Seamus Lysaght
Frontispiece photograph © Jessica Lysaght
The maps were compiled by Éadaoin Ní Néill

The lines from John Montague's poem *The Rough Field* (Section VI, 'The Source') are reprinted by kind permission of the Author's Estate and The Gallery Press, Loughcrew, Oldcastle, County Meath, Ireland from New Collected Poems (2012).

ISBN 978-0-9568918-6-0

Typesetting and layout by Sinéad Mallee

Printed in Ireland by KPS Colour Print Ltd, Knock, Co. Mayo

For Eleanor and Miguel de Eyto

Contents

Preface	17
Introduction	21
Maps	29
JANUARY	39
FEBRUARY	61
MARCH	77
APRIL	90
MAY	96
JUNE	109
JULY	123
AUGUST	142
SEPTEMBER	151
OCTOBER	167
NOVEMBER	197
DECEMBER	230
Notes	262

PREFACE

Unveiling the Sun: A Mayo Journal is a compilation of entries from notebooks and journals I have been in the habit of keeping for the last twenty-five years or so. These notebooks contain all sorts of occasional observations about moments and places that have caught my attention. The records include observations about weather, the progress of the seasons, plant life, hill-walking, animals and birds, fishing, mountains and uplands, and placenames. For several years, in the 2010s, this habit became a sort of discipline as I gathered experiences for two books, *Eagle Country* and *Wild Nephin*, published in 2018 and 2020 respectively.

This new volume is a selection of those journal entries compiled into one calendar year. This work was like an archaeological excavation: unearthing and cleaning old journal entries to see if they might still have some lustre, and reflect something of their original moment. By arranging them across the months and days of a single year, I relied on the seasons, with their patterns of change, to give shape to the overall series. In other words, I was looking to time, and not space, to supply the underlying narrative.

Many of these daily entries were written as short notes without any eye to publication and they still carry the innocence of private journal keeping (what the French call *écriture*); some others have a more deliberately literary accent, perhaps influenced by scenes I have described in earlier books, and from reading other writers whose work is structured around excursions into the outdoors. If nature writing has now become a branch of *littérature*, it is still haunted by the primal, apparently naïve *écriture* of its early influences.

As I gathered these scattered remains from their original handwritten pages, I discovered that some months were more abundantly represented than others. The record for some weeks was meagre; in a few cases there were gaps of several days in the calendar. I have mostly resisted a temptation to fill in these threadbare patches with extra darning and have left the gaps as they occur. The more extensive descriptions of some months, especially the winter months, suggest that as the days get shorter and the nights draw in, the impulse to write against the grain of winter's confinement gets stronger. In contrast, there were many exuberant summer days where journal keeping was neglected.

The heartland of this calendar extends from the drumlin landscape where I live outside Westport and encompasses the north Mayo area of the Nephin Beg Mountains and their surrounding river catchments. Over the years, I have shared my attachment to this countryside in many ways with many remarkable people. Michael Kingdon was my first companion exploring north Mayo's rivers and lakes over twenty years ago and he taught me much about the wildlife of that area. More recently I have spent memorable days walking the ground with Ged Dowling, Eleanor and Miguel de Eyto, Michael Chambers, Chris and Lynda Huxley, Digby and Alison Lewis, Colin Guilfoyle, Mark Wormald, Thérèse Ruane, John Harford and my wife Jessica. I am grateful to Jean-Pierre Maire and Nicola Stronach at the Ginger and Wild café in Ballycroy for their hospitality and generosity over several seasons, and to the staff at the National Park Visitor Centre in Ballycroy for many welcomes and ongoing support, especially Michael Chambers, Sinéad Gaughan and Fintan Masterson. Georgia Macmillan of the Mayo Dark Skies Park project has been a keen seconder of my own pursuits and I'm grateful to her for logistical help on a few occasions. William Maire's skill as an angler, as well as his

PREFACE

love of north Mayo's wild rivers, have both been an inspiration.

I am also indebted to people who have shared their knowledge or answered particular queries. Allan Mee, who manages the white-tailed sea eagle reintroduction project, supplied me with information about these birds in Mayo. The staff at the Marine Institute at Lough Furnace have given me much information about the Institute's research at Burrishoole. My conversations with Sam Birch, Sue Callaghan, Cameron Clotworthy and Denis Strong of the NPWS have been stimulating and enlightening, driven by our shared fascination with Wild Nephin. I should also like to acknowledge the expertise and generosity of contacts on social media who have responded to various queries, especially Lillis Ó Laoire, Barry Dalby, Barry Murphy, Michael Gibbons, and Gerard McGreal. Paddy Bushe and Aifric MacAodha helped me to navigate some unfamiliar Gaelic territory as I translated Féilim Mac Dhúill's poem 'An tIolrach Mór.' Éadaoin Ní Néill was a skilled collaborator as we worked on the maps for this volume.

Trisha Kuester read the draft text with generous, meticulous attention. The main task of editing fell to Jessica, who took to it with exemplary care. As is the case with *Wild Nephin*, the finished text owes a great deal to her good judgment and eagle eye for a careless phrase.

Finally, I'd like to express my gratitude and affection for all those people whose friendship over the years has made the remote places anything but lonely.

Westport, March 2025

INTRODUCTION

The road from Westport to Fahy runs through drumlin country, the landscape that forms the islands in Clew Bay. After a steep climb out of town with the imposing cone of Croagh Patrick behind me, I turn left into the Lodge Road to follow its undulations for about four kilometres as far as the half-parish of Fahy. Away to the north-west, the equally impressive bulk of Nephin sits like a target the road is aiming for.

Fahy itself is quite intensively farmed, though there are few dairymen left. Most of the fields around our house have been sterilised by the ways of modern farming to support subsidised herds of livestock. The heavy glacial clay of the soil, which is locally referred to as 'daub', was sweetened by the admixture of lime from local kilns: the clay sits on karst limestone, a fact that came home to me once when, on my way to Clogher Lough nearby, I discovered a stream which disappeared into the ground through a sink-hole. This bedrock was easily within reach of the quarrymen, who burnt it in kilns to produce lime.

Trees have traditionally had little or no role in farming around Fahy until modern forestry subsidies led to the planting of fragmented stands of sitka spruce. Only here and there, along the river valley at Brockagh, for instance, do you get a glimpse of native woodland in the bluebell-rich stands of hazel, birch and alder. The trees I planted around our house now constitute a kind of oasis among the tidy green fields of our townland, Lugnafahy. A line of black poplars planted about sixteen years ago for shelter from the westerlies is now screening one side of the site, depriving us of an earlier view towards north

Connemara. This reinforces my imaginative tendency to be drawn in the other direction, north towards Erris and the Nephins.

This northerly bias in the area is not unprecedented. In the old days, farmers went north to the townlands of Lappallagh, Derrintloura and Derrinumeera to cut their turf. As the bog was traditionally a dumping ground for cars, machinery and appliances, there is an officially sanctioned legacy for this practice in the old landfill site at Derrinumeera, now a recycling centre. The turf plots in this area are now largely abandoned, and because the patchwork of turbary rights prevents these lands from being reclaimed for farming, a rich succession of wild vegetation has returned, with an added element of feral conifers from the forestry.

This was the northern limit of my late neighbour Martin O'Donnell's world. He cut turf at Lappallagh, six kilometres to the north-east. He went to Westport for day-to-day needs, and occasionally to Castlebar, the county town. The mountains, bogs and forests that are the main subject of this journal were outside his normal experience and routines, though a few famous incidents from Ireland's rebellious history would have lived on in his imagination, and as a shrewd livestock farmer he had dealings with other men from all over the county.

In 2000, his son John built the house where we now live. At first, there was only a wire fence and a line of hawthorn slips to shield us from the elements, then a winter of fierce storms several years later prompted me to reinforce the boundary by planting black poplars. I also planted saplings on the lower, sloping portion of the site, including a job lot of oaks from a local nursery: these turned out to be pendunculate oaks (*Quercus robur*) and not the sessile oaks (*Quercus petraea*) favoured by nationalists. One of my students, a thatcher from Galway called Gerry Joyce, gifted me a bunch of seedling hazels which he had propagated in pots at his home at Annaghdown, near Headford. My father presented us with a Turkey oak (*Quercus cerris*) which now rivals a broadband pole near the entrance gate. Other trees were added haphazardly over the next few years: Scots pine, field maple, lime, beech, rowan, birch, alder, holly, hazel, ash; and some willow and sycamore grew naturally on ground that had been disturbed during the building. Mark Granier and I planted a line of beeches along the northern boundary, which we now refer to as the Granier Grove. Chris and Lynda Huxley brought several blackthorns, daffodils and a spindle from their property near Belcarra, outside Castlebar. Michael Kingdon brought gifts of arbutus and blackcurrant bushes. Eleanor de Eyto gave us gifts of smaller plants in pots. And now nature has taken over this work as oak, hawthorn, birch and hazel seedlings are starting to appear around the site.

While the trees were still small, grassy growth flourished on the lower part of the site, enclosed by a hedge of young hawthorns. In those days, meadow pipits from the big field next door often paid a visit and even nested for a couple of years. Once, as I cleared growth from around one of the oaks, I uncovered a grasshopper warbler's nest with young chicks and was dismayed when this hidden brood got predated after being exposed by me. As the trees matured, creating a shady canopy, the meadow pipits and grasshopper warblers abandoned the site; then it was the turn of willow warblers and blackcaps to move in. The willow warbler especially is a favourite of ours; its arrival with its song from Africa at the start of April marks the beginning of summer and is the soundtrack for long days until September. Another migrant that has recently shown a preference for the woodland garden is the spotted flycatcher, which hunts flies from high branches.

So our house is gradually settling into a wooded situation. The only disadvantage is that, as the trees grow, you lose the view, and the house is threatened by the encroachment of shade, a sad process in a climate where sunlight is at a premium. This means, in turn, that the poplars and oaks need to be cut back and pruned, a duty that is turning me into a true woodlander. Otherwise, with the trees unchecked, our house would be overwhelmed by a slow tide of foliage and shade, and become itself a kind of tree house within a green gloom in summer, with a noisy rookery to accompany us in old age. For the moment, as long as I can, I'm cutting back branches in order to stem the tide of complete rewilding at the house, and I favour the kind of woodland mixture that attracts blackcaps, willow warblers, and the common birds.

While Fahy and its managed fields are the setting for this woodland oasis, my adopted place has a wider reach northwards, encompassing the mountains, forests and bogs of Wild Nephin. Much of this area is within the National Park, whose boundary is marked on Barry Dalby's pioneering map of Wild Nephin as a pink broken line, but since that limit of outright ownership is invisible on the ground, the empire of the state merges seamlessly with forests and commonages nearby, and it operates no restriction over the range of curiosity and wonder recorded in these pages.

The territory explored by this journal extends from Mulranny in the west to Keenagh in the east, from Fahy in the south to the Corslieve massif at its northern limit; it encompasses the blanket bogs of the Owenduff and Tarsaghaunmore river catchments around Ballycroy, the coniferous forests to the east of the Nephin Beg Mountains, and the mountains themselves, stretching in a great arc from Mulranny to Bangor. I have been exploring this area for over twenty years, driven by a consistent, though domestically tolerable obsession, in the company of Jessica and others, or on my own; and while the bogs and forests of north Mayo can at times feel very empty of life, that desert-like quality appeals to me as a challenge: to populate what for many has been seen as a deadzone with observations of my own.

I count myself fortunate to live within an easy drive of mountains, bogs and forests; there are other places within nearer reach, such as the drumlin lake at Gorteen, or the Owennabrockagh River, which I can get to on foot. Without driving anywhere, I am surrounded by variety and interest in the woodland garden at our house. Between our own house and the remote bogs of Erris there's a kind of continuum, though within that the Wild Nephin area still exerts a special gravitational pull, away from the comforts of routine towards a place of challenge.

Wild places have played a part in our culture for centuries. Even the most urban societies have needed an outlet in hunting grounds and open spaces; long before romantic tastes brought genteel folk to wild scenery, European power elites knew the value of being able to roam unimpeded over royal forests, usually on horseback. In 21st-century Europe, computer programmers and financiers extol the value of the living world to their children and drive distances at weekends and on holiday to give themselves and their families direct experience of nature in wild places. The enormous flourishing of nature writing in Britain and Ireland since the 1970s is a symptom of a society increasingly enmeshed in digital technology for education, entertainment and employment, and removed from the living landscape as a workplace. That landscape has instead become a testing ground for ourselves as individuals, with our binoculars, our fitness monitors and heartbeat trackers, our stopwatches and smartphone cameras. Precisely what the meaning of 'wild' might be in this context is a moot point. (I am not concerned with political and conservation questions surrounding ideas of the wild at this moment.) At times I think that there are as many dramas being played out among the insects and mosses of my half-acre woodland as on the slopes of Corslieve (721m), and perhaps the day will come when I hang up my walking boots and concentrate instead on what a microscope can discover on a fragment of decaying wood from the woodland floor.

For now, though, there is both an emphasis on and a preference for remote places in north Mayo, whether I travel with binoculars, fishing rod, or notebook. The encounter with a favourite landscape is a two-way process (or perhaps it works three ways, if a loved one or friend is there as well). Knowing a landscape becomes a form of self-knowledge, as Robert Macfarlane has argued so persuasively and memorably in *The Old Ways* and *Landmarks* especially. A cherished landscape, as it is explored and celebrated, becomes a zone of unpredictable discoveries, a realm of potential not only for what it adds to general knowledge, but for what it reveals in ourselves. It is there, and only there, that we can encounter the forms that shadow us in our lives, and there that we come face to face with our latent capacities, our inhibitions, our destined impulses. At the same time, the place itself is changed in the process: as Nan Shepherd has put it, 'The thing to be known grows with the knowing.' Indeed, there are moments when the two, place and person, merge into a single insight, so that it becomes impossible to separate the two. When the angler Sidney Spencer wrote, about the nocturnal hunt for sea trout, 'The darkened river is another world, its sights are hidden, its scents and voices intensified,' he was being drawn into a realm of creative perception. With their licence to transform experience through metaphor and figuration, poets have traditionally occupied this space, but at moments of penetrating insight, the best prose writers can take us there as well.

Such moments of revelation are not granted every day to the walker, the watcher, or the hunter. In her search for goshawks in the Norfolk Brecklands, Helen Macdonald reckoned that the appearance of one of these elusive creatures was like a gift of grace: 'it comes, but not often, and you don't get to say when or how.' The same holds true for the eagle watcher in north

Mayo. You can look to the skies hundreds, perhaps thousands of times above the ridges of the Nephins and be rewarded once or twice, if ever, by the imperious kite of a sea eagle, or the more graceful span of a golden eagle quartering the hillside. Even where our western skies are desolate with memories of what used to be, a winter afternoon is redeemed by the appearance of a merlin flickering like an eye-mote across an upland valley. Scarcity creates value; forbearance and patience prepare the ground for the marvellous.

General Map of North-west Mayo

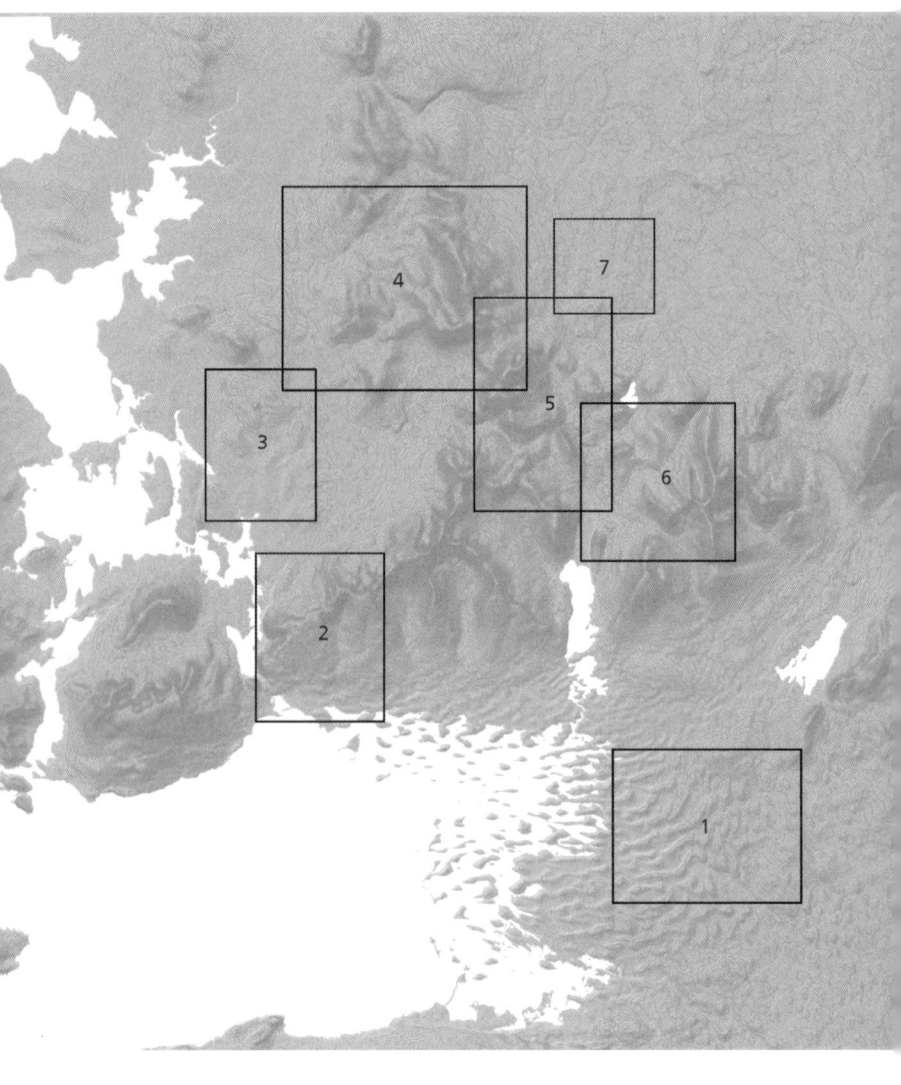

Area Maps

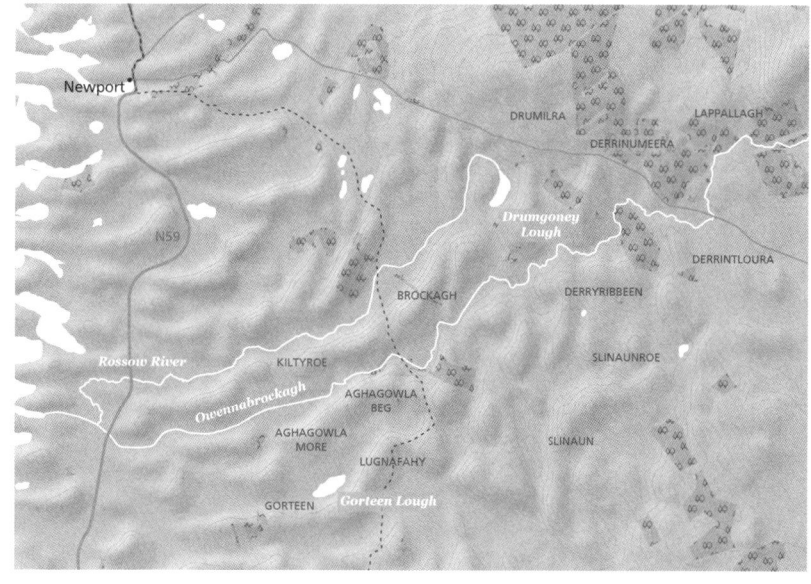

1. North of Fahy

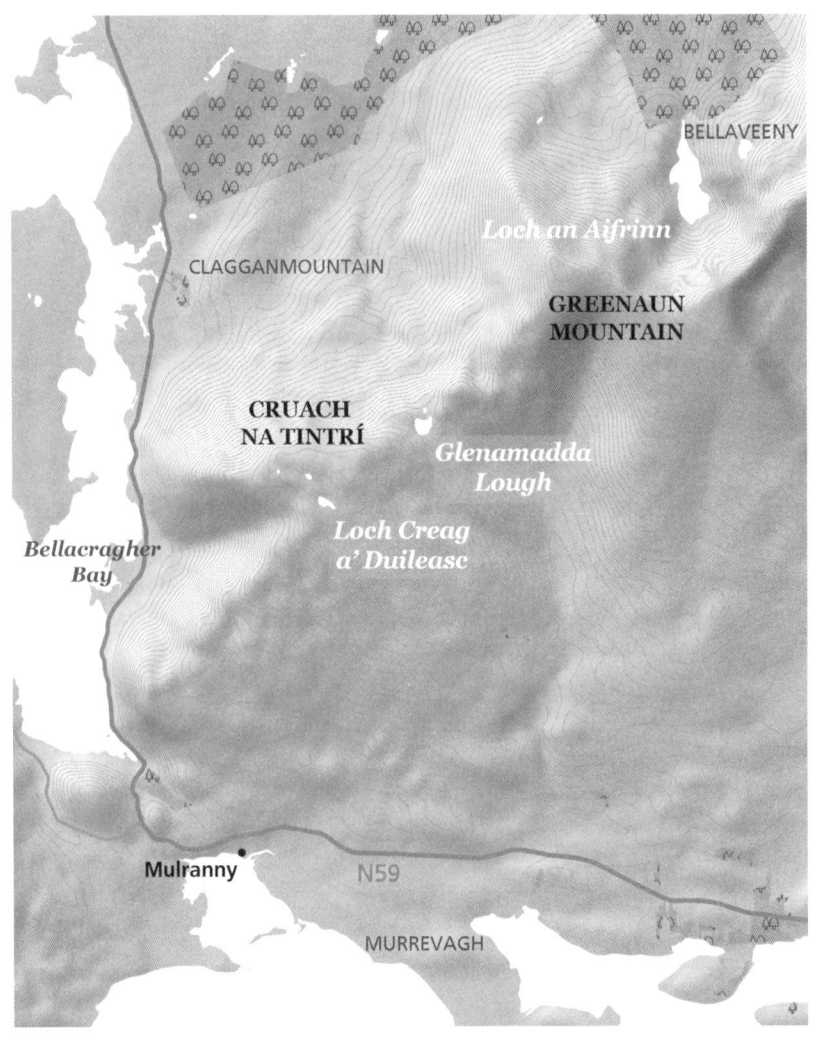

2. Mulranny and Claggan

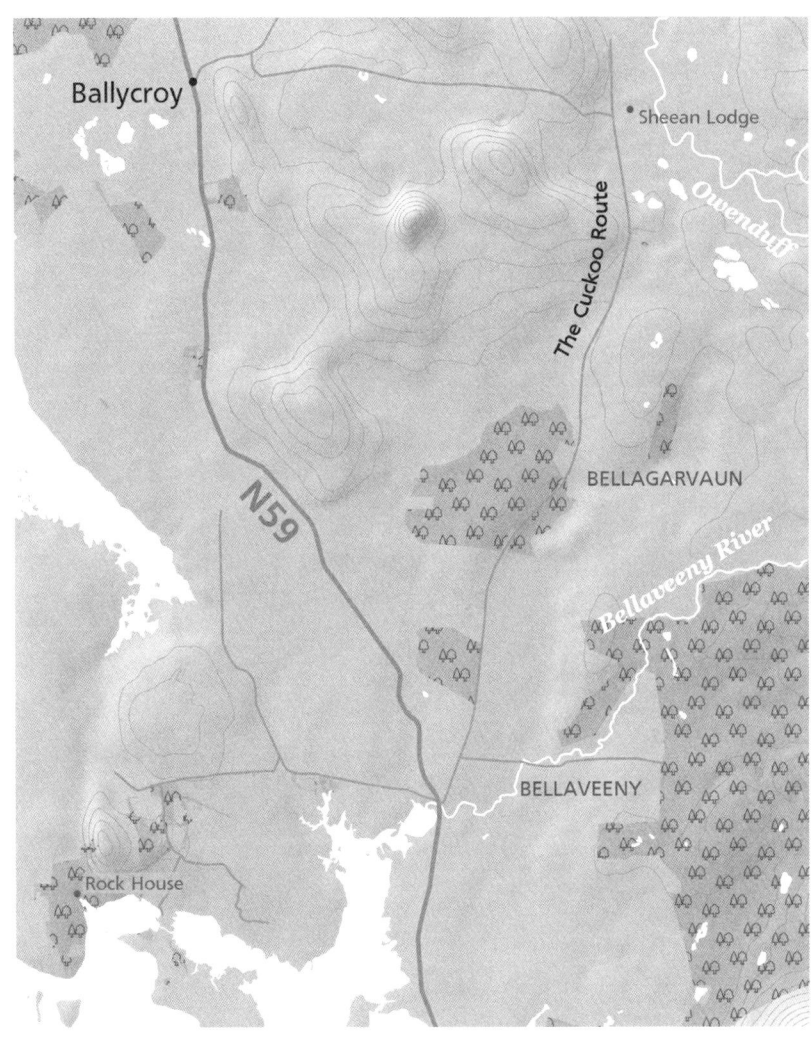

3. Ballycroy and the Cuckoo Route

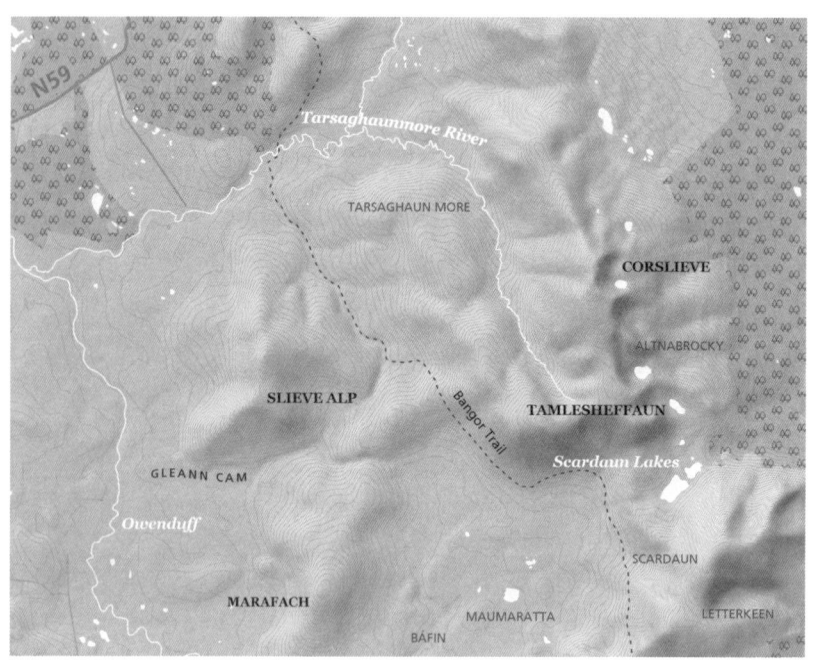

4. Owenduff and Tarsaghaunmore

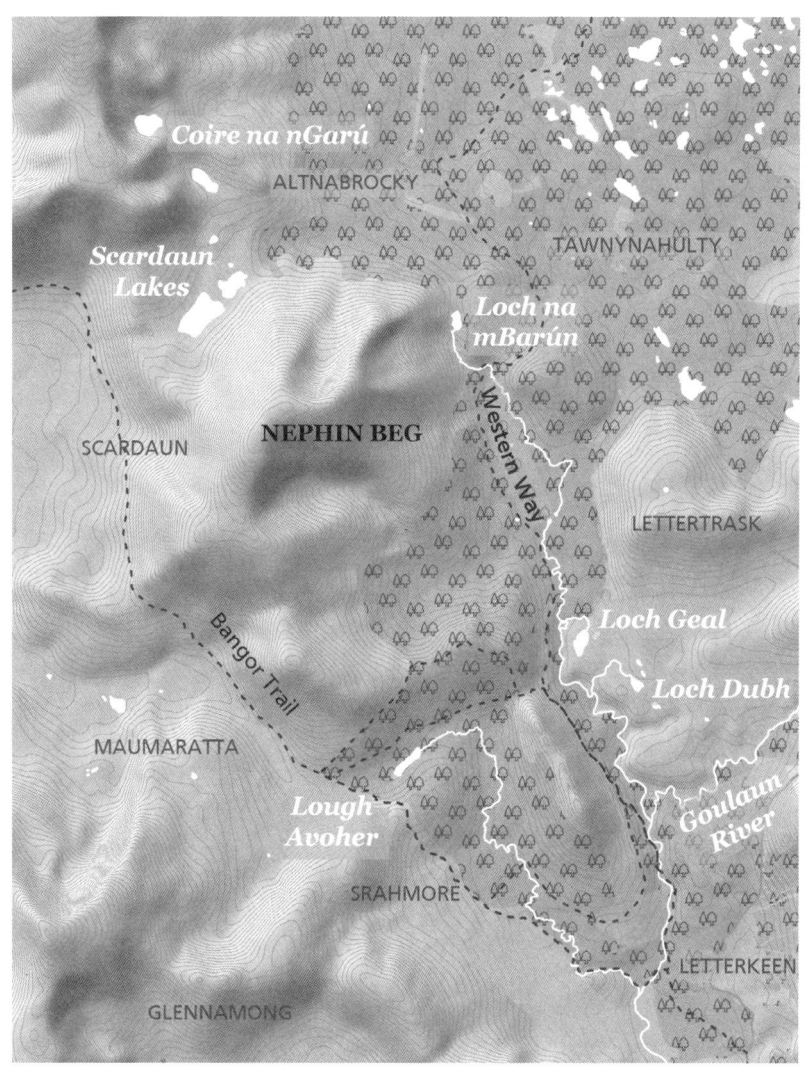

5. Letterkeen and the Western Way

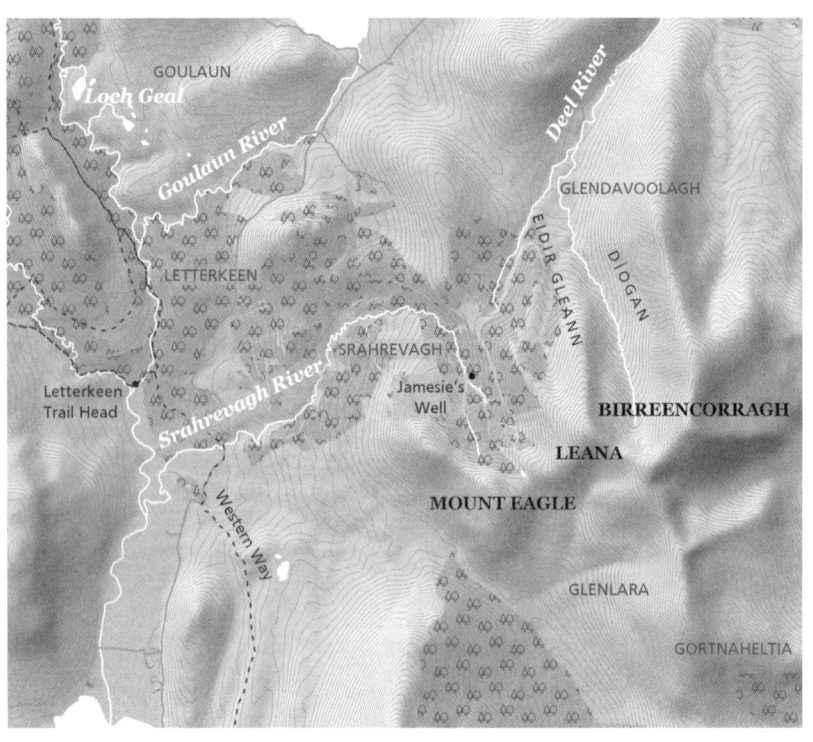

6. The Srahrevagh Valley

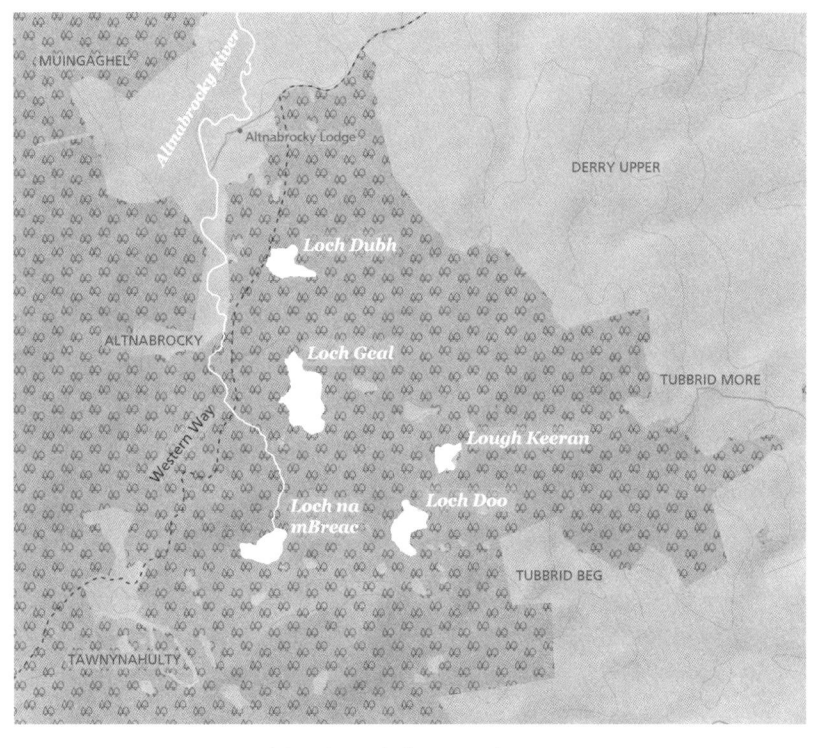

7. Tubbrid and the Nephin Forest

January

1st January

Lynda tells me over the phone that she and Chris saw a buzzard at Manulla on 29th December. This one, added to my own record earlier in the month, gives me optimism, a sense that this species is arriving in the west now. This joins forces with my expectations about sea eagles turning up in Mayo in future years as they continue to prosper in Scotland. I have almost finished Jim Crumley's book, *The Eagle's Way*, where he describes sea eagles in eastern Scotland moving west from the release site near Dundee on the Firth of Tay, to join up with birds from western populations in Mull, Skye, and elsewhere. In several beautifully focussed passages describing close encounters with eagles, Crumley's veneration of eagles approaches spirituality. He has a keen perception that eagles (golden and sea) are part of the wild essence of Scotland, along with the extinct wolf. He also describes historical sites in central Scotland, where sea eagles are being encountered again. 'Once an eagle rock, always an eagle rock', he insists.

2nd January

Lough Feeagh. I park overlooking the second bay where I saw an otter once, from the shore of Buckoogh. Steady rain, as loud on the car as rain you hear pattering on the wall of a tent, while you lie there, reluctant to move. Buckoogh, Crimlin and Torc Shléibhe just visible as brown-grey hills under cloud.

Colours: neon-green moss, pale touches of mat grass, spiky vertical strokes of green rushes, rusty old bracken plastered against the ground; somewhere in the grey murk, gorse holds yellow blossoms of hope or defiance; *Erica erigena* is bleeding lilac and mauve here and there.

I open the door briefly to hear a loose clattering noise (that's water too, not a loose sheet of metal) and am spotted with fresh water. The general greyness attenuates the surface of the lake – less visible agitation on its surface under the assault of raindrops.

Birch trees showing plum colour beside their white silvery trunks, like strips of fat beside mature meat.

Where mat grass (*Nardus stricta*) predominates, the ground has a bleached look, as if nutrition and life have drained out of the earth; molinia is a slightly warmer straw colour, but its leaves are paper-thin ribbons which fly away in gales and wrap themselves round branches and wires. (Swifts use this for nest material.) Deer sedge gives a warmer look, a tinge of chestnut or roan; bog myrtle lends a similar colour, often combined with molinia.

Black bog rush, deep green, ageing to grey (no warmth in its tone).

I go through the wire opening overlooking the mouth of the Glennamong River. What, people might wonder, is he doing there in this weather? An outlaw. To be classified with the republicans who trained here during the Troubles. No sign of any bird life in the bay at the river mouth. A lone runner passes, salutes.

Small streams flow down from the corrie under Bengorm, showing silver and white. The largest has a little river valley of its own, cutting through the dark slope. Its outwash forms a large wedge of ground, paler in colour than the rest. More mat grass and moss; the sediments make firmer conditions, less poached by animal hooves than the peat.

At first, the plantation in Glennamong looks like a dark green tsunami frozen for a moment as it charges down the valley. The river is turbulent and steely, showing white where it passes over stones; the foamy appearance is not constant, but wavering, as if the stones themselves were moving, like a run of salmon moving upstream. The river is a downward rush of gravity, also an upholding rush of stone staying put. Just the staying-put of the stones reveals the rushing agitation of water.

*

The stream is high, in brown spate, on my way back. A low sun almost appeared shortly before sunset, adding a yellow trace to the overcast sky, but the moment passed and rain closed in again.

When I got home, there was agitation high in the trees as storm Eleanor arrived. A brief affair, enough to knock out power for two hours. We ate supper by torch and candlelight; I lay down to be warm, the house was cold without heating. Jessica played the piano.

I said to Jessica how part of me hates these storms: they vandalise our terra cotta pots, make us shut the chimney (so no fire), knock us back to the 19th century without light. The raw wild element is opposed to our world. King Lear.

3rd January

Letterkeen. With Chris and Lynda. We drive to the Carroll bothy and take the Bangor Trail, then cross the fence onto the single-file pedestrian track through forestry. Everything is very quiet.

Unveiling the Sun

Almost nothing stirring in the plantation – a few coal tits and goldcrests. I point out the old golden eagle site to Chris and Lynda. We discuss the site at Mount Eagle, which I think was vulnerable to fox predation; Chris believes that eagles would have seen off the fox.

After the walk we drive to Lough Bunaveela. Chris would like to fish here when the season starts. Beautiful, isolated sheet of water with native hill brownies and bigger speckled trout.

A kestrel hovering over Letterkeen Hill.

5th January

Mark Granier and I go to Treanlaur to see the two-storey house, Sheehan's. It is colder than recently, somewhat overcast. The tops of Buckoogh and Bengorm are covered in cloud. Mark takes photographs. Sycamores were planted at the back, not at the front of the house, where they would have shielded it from the westerlies. Instead, they kept the view clear to Croagh Patrick and Clew Bay. No peasant in his cottage was ever interested in views.

Back at the car, we meet two local women who are pleased to see us and greet us warmly. The people who lived in the house were called Sheehan; they worked for the landlord, a Frenchman called Laprimandage. The older lady, who is now somewhat frail, lives in a house he built. We exchange warm wishes before we part company.

A lovely sheepdog, with a white and tawny coat, approaches us; its back is as narrow as a fox's.

We stop near Lough Feeagh to look at two very silvery trees growing in front of a copse of downy birch. The birch boles are a creamy pale colour, but the silver trees outshine them. I cross the fence to examine them – they are rowan – and discover that the silvery colour of the bark is enhanced by extensive patches of white lichen. There are no berries left now: the trees are resplendent in their abstraction.

We drive to Crossmolina after lunch in Newport. Much of Nephin is lost in low cloud. Mark takes more photographs. Evening light on the Deel River is soft grey, unruffled by wind; a few trout are darting about, making faint waves. A song thrush is in full voice in a tree beside the river. The town is immaculately kept, there must be an inspection in the near future. A plaque in the centre commemorates the thousands of people who worked for Bord na Móna harvesting peat in the past. What jobs are there in Crossmolina now?

At five o'clock, the mountains are still visible as we drive back to Newport. Mark mentions Janus, who looks two ways: one way is ahead, towards lengthening days. The count has already started.

6th January

Day length on 21st December: 7:29:55

Day length on 6th January: 7:44:57

About a quarter of an hour added.

The rate of increase accelerates through March until late April, when over four minutes are being added every day.

7th January

A soft day with almost no wind. I spent an hour cutting brambles. Catkins on the American alder are extended in the mild weather. I saw a little caterpillar on a strand of gossamer and caught it in my hand.

At dusk, a big sparrowhawk flew into the hazels, moved among the branches, and went off.

Unveiling the Sun

8th January

The morning is overcast, mild, and perfectly still. Song thrush singing. A group of long-tailed tits hunt insects in the oaks.

10th January

Mild, mostly wet days, with some breaks in the cloud. I have work to do at the desk and am not inclined to venture out. Reading Seton Gordon's book, *The Golden Eagle*.

11th January

The sun was a distinct disc just after sunrise, softened by a haze of thin cloud, trimmed of its glare. Then it was sleeved gradually into darker cloud above it.

Snow is forecast. The oaks behind the hedge were shaken by wind today as if a large animal were tugging at each trunk. When I went out to the shed a panic of redwings rose out of the willows and scattered down again. I managed a half hour of cutting between squalls, pecking at rush clumps like a crow in a pageant.

A few bluebell leaves are showing under the hazels, and the narcissi are in fresh bunches, soon to flower. Spring is already shaping its sub-plot within the winter weather: we are braced for snow overnight and tomorrow. I want to climb into its white world.

12th January

A little egret has been feeding in Gerry's field regularly for a few weeks.

13th January

Birreencorragh and Nephin very clear and white.

14th January

Murrevagh. We drove to Mulranny after breakfast to walk before midday, as rain was forecast from lunchtime. A brownish, juvenile sparrowhawk flew ahead of us along the road and disappeared round a corner. As we approached, it flew again from its perch, gliding very low, barely a foot above the road, and turned to perch on a branch, flying again along the road as the car came near. It did this five times before we eventually lost sight of it.

The previous evening another sparrowhawk had flown past me as it was getting dark, low across a field, very flat, thin and shadowy, like those military planes designed to evade detection by radar, an essence of concealment; that bird was barely an incarnation of a shadow in twilight. And still, it was enough to portend death to the redwings.

Wind was stirring in the tall spruce as we got near Mulranny. The links golf course was cropped very tight – it must be commonage – and had a peaty look in places where sheep hooves had poached the ground; the putting greens were green, as they are fenced off and sheep don't graze there.

Wind was brisk off the sea, almost a gale, wrapping the golfers tightly in their black weatherproofs. Gulls floated easily on the updraught off the brow of the dunes. Rough waves were a steady commotion at the beach, now exposed. We followed an otter's prints along the top of the beach, close to the stony margin. The animal had gone along the shore earlier that morning, and we followed its trail, tempted by the chance of a sighting. Two hundred yards of this, and the tracks came to an end: it dawned on me that at that point, the animal had entered the water, which must have been higher at that moment, close to where we were standing. We were left stranded in our land-bound state by this magician of water. Little hope was left of seeing it in the windy commotion of waves.

A few dozen dunlin and sanderling were feeding in the little bay around the corner. I was too tight in the cold to pause to count them. A single curlew took off 'like a guilty thing surprised'. It did not want to be questioned about its dramatic decline as a breeding species.

Deposits of rock, seaweed and plastic had been rearranged by storms since we were last here.

We turned inland at the extreme point and came back across the machair. A clean, fresh portion of fleece, with hooves and bones, was all that remained of a young sheep that had perished: the land itself had the appearance of a scavenged carcass. Life itself took on this extreme economy: a flock of small waders flew across, a brief glimmer of urgency, Shelley's 'thinnest boat', for the soul of January.

The standing stone, with a limestone cairn at its foot marking the children's burial ground, was the only thing that seemed worthy of a photograph. Life was a marvel today in the cold and penury, so its early extinction deserved to be respected and remembered. The infants buried here away from consecrated ground were miscarriages, stillbirths or infant deaths, consigned to Limbo without the passport of baptism. This heart of winter is itself Limbo, when there is scarcely a hope of new life stirring: the accent is on staying, being, surviving.

One chough trying to forage on a poached stretch of ground was an emblem of the place, its cracked voice like a fuller idiom worn thin by the territory. A worn-down jackdaw.

We paused on the brow of the dune to admire the lacework of waves, the darkness of stone which four brent geese had vanished into.

15th January

Lugnafahy. The other day, something red caught my eye on the ground ivy under the hazels – I wondered what kind of fungus had emerged in that familiar spot. A nearer look brought me to the breastbone of a redwing, recently stripped by a sparrowhawk.

Redwing like foraging under the oaks, turning leaves over in search of worms and slugs. But this is also the sparrowhawk's realm, so the redwing are usually skittish. They come into the willows and oaks in sudden flight from a sparrowhawk, unseen at first, perched somewhere in a hedge or on a fencepost. Starlings appear also, banking abruptly in tight, dense flocks of fifty or sixty, like a surfer's kite. When the sparrowhawk is moving, the redwings fling themselves into cover, or rise up over the house in skeins and constellations. Once they settle in the grey willows they are a difficult target for a sparrowhawk, the trees being so densely branched, but they make good views for my binoculars, and present clearly.

The weather is as unsteady as these birds being conducted by the hawk. Sun lights the bare, wet oak branches for a moment and warms my face in passing; then the sky darkens in a truculent squall. Trees and land are humming a tune to the Atlantic; it has been coming down from Iceland with the whooper swans for so many years that even the stones know it by now.

16th January

Reading Roger Deakin makes me crave more contact with outside, so I opened my window to let the song of a thrush into the study. It sang in the late afternoon right into dusk until darkness.

17th January

Spoke on the history and heritage of Mayo eagles at Westport

Unveiling the Sun

Coast Hotel. During questions, the issue of persecution and sheep farming scarcely came up. A good turnout, about sixty to seventy people. One man told me about an eagle he had seen near Bilberry Lough, pursued by a swarm of corvids.

18th January

John O'Donnell and a Polish man came to replace fence posts along the boundary of the site. I cut back branches with the bow saw and hand shears to allow them to get to the fence. Here and there, a few leaves already showing in the willow, and little red eyes on the hawthorn where the buds are inclined to swell before opening. We didn't need coats and worked in our pullovers. The poplars looked very clear and silver, lit from the west against a backdrop of grey sky.

John tells me that foxes are very plentiful, especially in the forestry. There's one fox that comes round his house every night, prospecting. The fox will kill lambs for sport, and may only eat part of the head, or remove part of a lamb's jaw to chew on the mandible.

We talked about lambing out on the mountain. One man, whose father was ill in hospital, did not bring his ewes down from the mountain, and they lambed up there, with very few losses.

The fence posts John used were from Sweden, specially treated with creosote so that they don't rot. The Irish product is poor by comparison, he tells me, and are inclined to rot at the foot after a few years. A farmer he knows got €10,000 worth of these for a fence across the mountain near Leenane; he paid for a helicopter to ferry the posts up onto the mountain where they were being put in.

I planted some daffodils which Chris had given me from his site. They are the same as the wild variety.

The Polish man cut down the remaining willow trunks on our site with a chainsaw.

19th January

I set out to check Gorteen Lake for whooper swans. (I had seen eight a few days earlier, when the lake was full after a very wet spell.) An earlier squall of hailstones had passed; a keen wind from the NW was whetting the bare, sharp stone of winter. I walked up the steep drumlin to the old ring fort, with only the steep grassy slope as a horizon above me. Going zigzag, I gradually lifted the Nephin Beg Mountains into a grey sky. Although the ground was wet and soggy at my feet, the cheek-freezing wind brought its own signal of white purity from the north. The ridge of Glendahurk was being swallowed by another grey squall; the same cloud-cover was dissolving Buckoogh, Mount Eagle, and Birreencorragh; only the pyramid of Nephin stood out white and pristine: snow and hail had blanketed the slopes, there was no peppering of heather coming through: up there now was a shout-echoing abstraction of white, all the way to the summit at 800 metres.

Once I got to the very top of the whaleback drumlin and took its full exposure, it was as if there could be no standing there, 'no abiding stay', but I still raised my binoculars and counted four whooper swans at the far side of the lake, feeding in shallow water. There were four more in the narrow channel of the outflow.

Several years ago, numbers were double that: I used to see about sixteen in one of the long fields on the northern side, but fence improvements since then, and probably a degree of disturbance at one of the flock's other haunts, have made this area less attractive. Whoopers like pasture, but they need to be able to reach the safety of open water quickly, and the big modern fence at the edge of the lake has not suited them.

One June day in 2004, I picked up a yellow plastic ring in that long field with the code 4PX, and sent my record to the authorities. The swan that lost it had been ringed as a cygnet at Skagafjörður in northern Iceland nine years earlier. Ornithologists had spotted the coded bird during the next few summers at the same breeding grounds; then it was seen at Lough Swilly in County Donegal in late autumn 1999 and 2000 on its way to Mayo for the winter.

Having checked the lake for other wildfowl – a few mallard, teal and little grebe – I walked towards the shelter of a ditch topped with gorse and stood in its lee, with a look-out over the six-acre body of water. The swans had stopped feeding when I appeared on their horizon, did their stiff-neck-to-attention pose, and then relaxed to feed again. Now, as I followed them with binoculars, they were moving sedately close to the shore, heading to the western end. Their appearance was laundry-white on grey water, but their necks were still a warm buff colour, stained by volcanic silt in the Icelandic waters where they feed in summer.

Whooper swans return to our area in October, a heavy, jet-plane approach accompanied by their wheezy peals, as if an old accordion struggled to make up a tune from only two notes. Weather and the search for food displace them throughout the winter, and they put in regular appearances over the house, like lost souls, or Lir's children clamouring for release.

With eight whoopers in my chronicle for this late January day, I did not need to linger. A few gulls and corvids were loitering around the sheep feeder at the bottom of the slope; two other gulls were sliding easily along the updraught from the drumlin where I stood. This muddy hollow near the lake, where the ground was poached from the impact of hooves, was like the 'black hills' in Kavanagh's poem 'Shancoduff', which 'have never seen the sun rising'.

I started to go back. Each of my steps across the top of the drumlin left a muddy boot print: my neighbour would find an exact record of my hesitations and meanderings the next time he crossed the drumlin on his quad with a bale of fodder, just like Kavanagh's poor poet.

My steps brought me down from that altar of cold, through the windscreen-shatter of hailstones. The first scatterings of another squall just caught me as I got back to the porch of my house.

20th January

A calm, overcast day. From the study I can see the straggling line of the escallonia hedge with the other plantings: whitethorn, pine, oak, field maple, sycamore. Only the oaks still hold leaves from last year; the winds have stripped the last yellow tassels from the willow: the new buds are downy, silvery. First to venture into the new year's growth is the elder: two daisy-sized shoots have emerged to tempt the end of winter.

22nd January

Gorteen Lough. 11.00-13.00. Eight whoopers still present. Five ladybirds on a fence post. A little egret in the flooding at O'Donnell's side. Twenty-five teal.

I came across fifteen pied wagtails feeding on very muddy ground at the bottom of O'Donnell's; these are presumably the birds that roost at the lake, in the reeds.

I crossed the fence to the next property, lots of brambles, willow scrub, and hazel. Honeysuckle starting to show. A woodcock crashed out of the ditch at the hazel corner, just as expected.

A pair of little grebe calling together at the western end, then diving to feed. A well-bonded pair already. The screech of a water rail in the willow thicket at the western end. Very loud.

The whoopers (four at the eastern end) were very nervous of me approaching on foot. They soon joined the other four in the flooding to the west, where they tolerate vehicles passing noisily along the road.

A sparrowhawk about, sending jackdaws and rooks into the air; they take no chances.

The old willow very stark against the grey sky, Fay Godwin-like.

I walked slowly, dawdling along; this was the nearest thing January has to a spring day.

25th January

Corraun, with William Maire. One of those late-winter days, when the old regime of cold, and angry storms, is being challenged by a new angle of the sun's light, and the unassuming progress of honeysuckle shoots and daffodil leaves.

Sea trout was our target, to catch these in salt water, where they spend most of their lives, apart from their late summer appointment with freshwater streams to spawn. The fish we were after are big, running to four or five pounds, and are a much paler colour than the steel-and-smoke counterparts we meet from July onwards in the bog pools.

William has lived most of his life away from the city, in Connemara, West Mayo and – as a student – in Scotland. A passionate angler in fresh and marine water, he has supplied me with neoprene overalls and boots to allow me to stand in the frothing waters and get nearer to our quarry.

Our route took us along the northern coast of Clew Bay, as the aftermath of recent storms was still working big waves against the rocky shore – the kind favoured by surfers, which peel away steadily in one sideways movement, forming a smooth loop for the riders. The water was a pale duck-egg green, a chalky tone, but as the waves lifted and peaked, the waters stretched up to a blueish glitter, crested with a rocket-blast of spindrift, and crashed forward to a rush of foam. Clew Bay was keeping this wave a secret today: only one battered surfer's van was parked at Pink Rock, the favoured spot.

We drove to the south-west corner of the peninsula, which looks out towards Clare Island and the southern tip of Achill. Tidal waters surge through the channel between Corraun and Achill, forming very strong currents: the backwaters close to the main current are where sea trout might be loitering, feeding on sand eels.

Once I have squeezed into my neoprenes and tight boots, I feel more astronaut than angler, but this is the right armour for January: some squalls are forecast ahead of a clearance in the afternoon.

We walk to the dunes, skirting a sandy bay with its sentries of redshanks raising the alarm. The air is unsteady; we are buffeted by cold gusts; 200 yards away, big breakers are raising manes of spray to over twelve feet. Away to the west, through the narrow gap between Achill and Achill Beg, a great commotion of water is smashing into the shallows – the Atlantic hammering at the door. But the land won't let it in. In all this movement of air and water, the rocks and sands hold steady, and the low-slung kayaks of shags patrol the margins of the flow streaming past us: the tide is falling.

Big, rounded boulders of red sandstone arranged along the beach are a wet, gleaming liver-brown: the waters break to a white foam and then drag muddy suds back into the following wave.

We cast our sand eel imitations into the sea and retrieve quickly, hurrying them back along the weedy fringe of the shore. After an hour, we have struck nothing, and move farther around the corner to the next point, where a gang of shags give way reluctantly and relaunch into the current. Although this is a wild extremity, the harbour of Cloghmore is on the other side, with its industrial huddle of fish-processing units and boat-maintenance yards. As we were fishing, a nameless trawler steamed up the channel to the pier, making steady headway against the current, demonstrating the mastery of the machine.

William took a few photographs of me fishing, with the surge and slip of foam water spread in front of me. Clew Bay was under a grey tarpaulin of cloud, the ridge of Croagh Patrick in the distance like the rim of teeth in a turtle's jaw. The needle line of my upheld rod a pointed certainty, holding steady in the commotion of water and air.

We retreated to the car for a sandwich and watched a restless flock of curlew fussing across the top of a field thirty metres away. Their bills probed the grass like unwieldy medical devices; a few redshanks tagged along as well, following their larger cousins. We chatted about Scotland and the salmon season, which started on the Tay in mid-January: seasoned old-timers in plus fours and deer stalkers pouring a wee dram into the water as a piper played to honour the spring fish. We envisaged something similar at Corraun: a libation of whiskey, and the Mulranny pipe band wheezing and droning in the rumble of breakers.

We returned for another hour, firing our spinners into the unsteady, heaving meniscus just beside the current, with a few onlooker seals. We each had one pull from a fish, a tug at the line and the swirl of a large fish in the churning water close to the shore. These small plucks of life out of the cold element were enough to give meaning to the trip.

A man appeared on the crest of the dunes; he and I chatted for a while. Our conversation had many of the threads common to this place: exile and homecoming, the tedium of routine, a desire to forge a deeper, cultural relationship with this place, something we always seem to miss, to shoot wide of. Life as an accumulation of distractions, in cities, elsewhere, when the main prize is right here in the shore at our feet and the abiding loyalties of a few local families still continuing in cottages around us, where the Irish language lives on in a quiet way.

The crashing sea continued, performing its own baseline, nagging at all culture.

27th January

Miguel shows me snowdrops in his garden. Fresh leaves of mont bretia are like green flames along the roadside.

The light this morning is still a winter light, clear and clinical, but it is suffused with new awareness as we approach 1st February, St Bridget's Day. The salmon have spawned and the spent kelts are dropping back downstream. Hazel catkins are extending. Honeysuckle leaves are appearing. Someone in the south has seen the first frog spawn. New life is stirring.

I park at Letterkeen and walk out along the Western Way. Drizzle threatens for a while and then passes. When I stop after an hour to eat a snack, there are flies in the air beside me and I realise that my thick puffer jacket is much too warm today.

I turn left at the end of Correen More and climb the rocky trail of the Letterkeen Loop. Loch Geal and Loch Dubh are two panels of light on the wet bog, among other smithereens of bog pools.

This view of Loch Geal is one of those places where feeling is focussed, as if the lake were a lens for perception. It is here, as the view to the north opens up, that you see the first remnant of flow country, a great habitat that was substantially destroyed by afforestation, though some tracts remain. This is where I mourn an irreversible loss of scarce and valuable habitat to forest cover.

Unveiling the Sun

This makes Loch Geal like one of those *utamakura* of Japanese tradition, a place with very old, traditional associations, where a poet, say, once celebrated a moment and composed a poem (*waka*), and established a link that later poets would recognise. Their own poem at the spot would often quote or reference the old association. Loch Geal is such a spot for me, along with its obscure partner, Loch Dubh.

I have climbed up here today.
Loch Dubh is nothing darker
than Loch Geal –
because I am lighter.

I used to speculate that Loch Dubh was so called because of higher peat banks around its margin, but from the view I have today, that does not look right. The banks of both lakes look similar. Dubh – dark – perhaps just because it is hidden away, less immediately apparent.

I take the trail through the plantation leading to the top of Correen Beg. The plantation here, over thirty years old, is heavily festooned with *Rhytidiadelphus* moss. This moss covers the lower branches and trunks with a wispy, beard-like covering, which looks dry and sere at first, but in the hand lens appears like a glassy braid glistening with moisture.

When I leave the trees and cross open ground to get to the summit, the variety of moss, grass and sedges is a treasure. I rehearse, without fully mastering, some of the scientific names: *Racomitrium*, *Ulota*, *Rhytidiadelphus*, *Sphagnum*.

The summit, at 311 metres, offers a great panorama. Nephin is a gaunt, grey presence draped in scree, almost an abstraction at this remove. The valley between me and Nephin Beg is a patchwork of recent clear-fell with fresh track marks, new lodgepole planting, and a small area of broadleaf protected with plastic sleeves. Overgrazed hillsides to the south glisten with surface water where rain runs off bare peat. George Monbiot's term 'sheepwrecked' comes to mind.

A flock of about twenty meadow pipits at the edge of the bonsai pines: there must be enough insect life here for them this winter. If no frost comes in the next few weeks, these hardy little creatures will be first out on the bog, singing and setting up territories. There are so few creatures stirring in the forest today that anything is special: robin song, wren churr, chimes of a coal tit, raven pronk.

After the summit at Correen Beg, I drop down to return to the lower track. The going is easy through an old stand of lodgepole that has not thrived. The trees are gaunt and stark, with thin, black boles and meagre tufts of needles. Perhaps forty years old, they are starved survivors of the original plantation scheme. Most of them will eventually die off, leaving a few knotty veterans. This more open, varied aspect of the forest is pleasing.

At the edge of the plantation, overlooking the track, the sun is shining, and there's shelter. There's a stream to give me water for tea, so I stop and light the stove. The sound of running water plays strange tricks with my senses. I imagine I hear walkers' voices approaching from the east, but no-one appears. Even a curlew note bubbles up briefly through the trickling sound, but that too is an illusion.

The valley to the south is bounded by the long ridge of Correen More and the Bangor Trail. My little stream, along with the outflow from Lough Avoher, is part of this catchment; they feed into the Altachuiney stream, a tributary of the Srahmore River.

I pack up my stove and cup and step off the track to follow the stream; it tumbles through a series of white-water steps before turning south to meander across the bog, where it forms loops and pools, with fish-friendly gravel beds. (Elvira tells me there are no spawning salmon here, and thinks it's 'too acidic'.) For the last kilometre of its existence, this stream has a completely different character, which I see more clearly than ever today. Here it runs through a narrow cut it has made in a large moraine studded with big boulders; the gradient here is quite steep, with none of the leisurely pools and runs of the upper section. The stream hurries down, and has to negotiate many rocky obstacles as it goes; it divides and re-unites, briefly pours into bath-sized pools, and then runs past, or over large rocks once again. Today the river is not high, but still keeps its lively character. In times of heavy water, this delightful stream bubbles and fizzes with the exuberance of champagne; algae on the boulders gives the waters a greenish tinge.

28th January

A morning drive to Dublin for the Irish Raptor Study Group conference. A low sun in my face or just to the right for much of the way. Young ash trees along the road, their trunks wet from overnight rain: they flare as streaks of glister in the light. Alder reflect the light as well, but birch do not. Their pale trunks do not reflect sunlight, so they are obscure this morning, relegated to dullness while the alders and – especially – the ash are resplendent, servants of Bridget if not the goddess herself.

29th January

Went into the neighbour's field and walked along the river to check the fox den – no sign of any activity, as I expected. Primrose leaves showing, also leaves of cow parsley and vetch. The hawthorns along the river are collapsing, taking sections of riverbank with them. Great bundles of twigs and debris are held up by their branches.

A flock of pied wagtails stopped on the poached turf, calling, and then flew off towards the trees beside McHugh's cottage. They must have a roost over there. Jackdaws and rooks on the treetops, like Christmas lanterns, before they all rush off towards Westport in the dusk.

30th January

Lots of wreckage at Brockagh, where a beautiful thicket was destroyed last week by a big machine. Nothing left for the blackcaps, sedge warblers, willow warblers and grasshopper warblers that came here every summer. Jessica is very upset and vows not to go this way again. The frenzy of clearance is already underway, and is set to last until the end of February, when a seasonal ban on hedge cutting comes into force. This, at a time when we are celebrating the returning spring. Someone forgot to tell the big machines and their operators. The public rhetoric about sustainability is a joke, when in the engine rooms of the CAP and of local authorities nothing has changed.

Michael Chambers and Fintan Masterson have set up a desk in the bothy at Letterkeen, where Michael is making St. Bridget's crosses. He has made several, in two forms: the traditional four-branched cross, and the three-branched type, which occurred in a few northern counties.

The day is overcast and drizzling as Jess and I set out, going upstream towards the Monterey pines. Several spruce trees have sprouted from a fallen pine trunk, where they are secure from browsing deer and sheep. Eventually, as the log disintegrates and collapses, these young trees should gain a root-hold in the ground.

The river is low and clear. Where, I wonder, are the salmon that die after spawning? I have never seen any dead fish. Old Paddy McHugh did not believe that salmon died after spawning. Anglers catch plenty of kelts, or spent fish, in the early weeks of the angling season.

We get to the old forestry hut and make tea. Rain gets heavier as we stand in the doorway, eating our sandwiches. A storm system is crossing Scotland today, and we are within the swing of its tail, so the wind picks up. We attempt the rocky path at the end of Correen More in steady rain, with streams of water pouring over the rocks of the trail; as we climb, the wind comes in sudden gusts, and I worry that one of us might be pitched over onto jagged stones, so we take the decision to turn back, and return the way we came, along the eastern track under Correen More.

Streams and culverts are now full of watery sound; the river at the camping place seems louder than it was an hour earlier.

It's a head-down march back to the car, except that I come face to face with a large, yellow frog in the middle of the track. He is the best possible bearer of spring tidings on this wet, mild day.

Michael and Fintan are still at the bothy when we get back, and are demonstrating how to make crosses to a woman and her two young children. There's a row of freshly made, gleaming crosses lined up on the mantelpiece. We come away with two more as gifts for friends.

31st January

'What a fantastic January,' said Jessica.

1st February

At 7.15 a.m. the super blue full moon hanging in sycamore branches above Lavelle's, not like Heaney's flat host, but a deeper light, like the light in the recess of a torch's head, glowing strongly. A steam-train of cloud crossed, and passed; then an inky, moving promontory covered it; finally, a dense-smoke grey of cloud-tide rose over it and hid it in the hedge.

Moon: Super=second full moon of the month

      Blue=closest to earth

2nd February

With Eleanor to Jamesie's Well. The morning very mild and overcast. We park at the Srahrevagh stream and walk up the track into the old plantation. A mistle thrush is repeating his simple motif, a welcome early sign.

    Eleanor needs support getting through the squashy places. I take her hand to support her, or she slips her arm around my elbow, so I become her chaperone. Then we totter across a stream and sit in the gloom of spruce trees, to share an orange.

Another mistle thrush is singing in the valley at the wells. We drink water from all three springs and toast the health of our bodies. As there is no traditional ritual associated with these springs apart from drinking the water, we discuss what a new ritual might be. I am in favour of building a spa cabin using local forest timber and having hot baths and massage tables.

Everything bespeaks constant moisture, including the tussocks of moss that we sit on to eat our lunch. Drifts of low cloud move across Leana above us. There's the sound of water pouring from the pipes that have been lodged in the ground to channel the spring water, as well as the noise of two streams converging at the old booley hut. Water as a gift, an abundance here.

We come down along the stream past the ruined hut at the confluence and continue on, looking for a narrow part of the forest that will take us back to the track. We thread our way through, among magnificent spongy mats of vivid green sphagnum, and shaggy draperies of *Rhytidiadelphus*. Even rhododendron adds something of character with the wet lustre of its foliage: the bushes are scattered thinly through the plantation here and do not dominate.

Sheep, badgers and foxes have traced discreet networks of paths through the forest: we follow a trail among the trees running parallel to the main firebreak, breaking many pulpy, decayed branches as we go. This is quite exhausting work, and it's a relief to re-emerge into the open.

Eleanor is pleased with her achievement, getting to the well today, having failed to reach it once before. At seventy-seven, she is having to recognise certain limits; at sixty-four, I am feeling that I have limits too. Beyond all the palaver about age being just a number, I'm for a more prosaic approach to these outings: you plan a little, arrange to have time, and take your time.

Two ravens quarter the grove of big conifers at the top of Glen Augh, showing signs of getting ready to breed. They should be on eggs soon. I remember this fact from my first bird book, the *Observer's Book of British Birds*.

Drizzle comes on thickly as we get back to the car.

4th February

Emerson said that a fact in nature taken by itself is simply science, whereas a fact in nature allied to a human meaning is poetry.

5th February

My hawthorns are showing no signs of growth yet. Earlier this week in County Down, I saw tender new shoots of hawthorn in a park close to the sea. I used my new billhook to clear old growth from the base of the hawthorns. Water froze in basins last night, but the day was mild enough as I worked, the hollow swept by an occasional shower. Large, mixed squadrons of redwing and fieldfare whistled and chatted in the air above me, or landed in the fields below as if to discuss the terms of an elaborate strategy. Later on, starlings gathered in the tall beech trees sounded like a cascade, with sporadic whistles jumping from the stream of undifferentiated sound.

A sheep has died in the long field; its carcass lies in the middle of the flat, attended by two ravens and a gang of hoodies. The other sheep have deserted the flat and occupy the top part of the slope.

The sky at 5:30 is a lid of grey cloud with one break at the horizon around Maumtrasna. A pale apricot background sets the plateau in silhouette.

Heavy drops of mild rain as it gets dark.

7th February

The fields in the hollow below me have a milky covering of frost, and the hedges still cast long shadows. The farthest distance is made up of low ridges and tree-lines with the texture of aquarelle in an early mist.

10th February

Drifts of cloud on blue, with golden sunlight briefly on Buckoogh and Birreencorragh. From Glen Hest, these mountains look like a recumbent female figure, though with a modernist twist that makes it unclear which is shoulder, knee, thigh or hip. It's enough to tantalise on a cold February day, like a warm, voluptuous secret.

My friends R. and B. inherited a farm and cottage in Glen Hest and moved here permanently from London. They have extended the old cottage into a spacious, modern house and are now renovating some more buildings on the site, including an old granary, which gleams white with its fresh coat of paint. The farm contains the remains of a clachan settlement, a cluster of cottages and shelters within a crazy-paving pattern of small fields, paths and tracks. These are divided by imposing walls, much of them formed of stacks of quarried limestone.

R. and B. show me the old granary, which they started to renovate during lockdown. A large joiner's saw on its bench occupies most of the room; the work is still in progress; an iron winding staircase in the corner takes us to the upper floor, the granary of old, where potatoes and oats were stored. A cast-iron stove and a low ceiling suggest the warmth and comfort of an artist's mansard.

We leave the granary and continue along a track, climbing to the crest of an esker, where we get a view of the rest of the holding running all the way to the forested lower slopes of Birreencorragh. Rain threatens from the west as a grey turbulence dissolves Buckoogh and advances on the western flank of Birreen. R. tells me that Peregrine O'Cleary, one of the four master annalists, came to this area and died here. The bleak terrain of this February day, and the small hovels that now lie in ruins around us, hardly foster any kind of scholarship, let alone civilisation. This contrast, between precious philology and material dispossession, is familiar, but it is the first time I have felt it so keenly in a Mayo setting.

R. wants to plant some woodland here in a hollow area two fields away. As we look at the undulations of glacial drift, with their pelt of molinia, deer sedge and reindeer moss, we list tree species – birch, holly, hazel, guelder rose – like poker players revealing cards in a game of arboreal challenge. The townland name here is Gortnaheltia, where Peregrine O'Cleary lived his last twenty years; R. suggests that this means 'the field of the doe'; 'eilteog', I discover in Dinneen's dictionary, can also mean 'any little flighty thing'. Since I enjoy bending the mysteries of Irish placenames to my own purposes, I prefer to think of the name applying to the skylarks, pipits and warblers that will populate this place with their songs and doings in two months' time.

My admiration for this rough ground, in such contrast to the drastically managed grassland in my own area, is tempered by the cold squall that now catches us out. We turn back towards their house, still chatting about farm subsidies and the relentless pace of destruction of the countryside. One of their sheep has ended up alone in a field, separated from the flock. We turn her out and B. guides her back through a maze of walls and fences until she rejoins the rest. Such is the standard of scrutiny of land nowadays from the Copernicus satellites that a lone sheep in a field might get noticed by the agricultural inspectors who monitor compliance.

R. points to a stretch of forest in the distance. 'They shot a stag one morning over there. Hunters from Dublin. A friend of mine, a photographer, was visiting, he had a telephoto lens.' 'Did he get a picture?' 'Yes, you can see them dragging it by the antlers. That was a few years ago.'

Back at the house, I am invited into an annexe where R. brews his own stout, and I savour a small glass of the foaming beer. The unaccustomed taste of grain and ferment is a fitting antidote to the exposure of the day. Afterwards, the three of us sit over tea next to their generous windows, with portrait views of Lough Beltra and Croaghmoyle. A copy of the OS 6" map from 1836 is unrolled on the table, with corn kilns marked in pink post-it slips. Corn meant oats and oat-meal, and perhaps rye: crops for nourishment, thatching and the precious warmth of alcohol.

11th February

Squalls of hail, snow and rain have been falling for days. The weather map shows white ovals in clusters coming off the Atlantic, meaning snow – though some of it falls as rain at lower levels.

We drove to Mulranny through intermittent hail. The mountains were white shapes rising into a smoke of cloud. Wind seared the land from the north-west.

As we left the car at the railway bridge, I saw a shape swimming away through the standing water among the trees – a frog: dark clots of spawn formed a toadskin on the water surface; the spawn was being swayed by the movement of orgy revellers below the surface.

The first stretch of the Greenway heading to Achill is sheltered in the old rocky-sided cutting, rich with ferns and with water dripping from the sides. Bellacragher Bay appears through the old birches: a broken surface of water with salmon cages. The escarpment of Claggan Mountain looks down on the bay with the pride of its designation as a peregrine site, though there are no peregrines here today. And no otters to be seen on this rough water. The holt is deep in the embankment under us.

Farther on, the vista opens up gradually as we pass the farmstead obliging the Greenway to make a brief detour from the old railway. The birches are old and charactersome: vellum-white boles with spoke-explosions of growth and dense clusters of witch's broom. The twigs form a rich, wine-coloured canopy here covering old fields, enclosures and cultivation ridges – a history preserved under the mosses and sedges of a damp woodland floor.

Just past the farm, a strong brook off the mountain cascades and skitters over rocks under the path and continues its fall to the sea, where it gives the otters a reliable source of freshwater to wash the salt out of their fur.

Despite the rough conditions, we search the shore with binoculars, still haunted by the otter we watched in this place swimming and diving directly under us some months ago. The main entertainment today is supplied by gulls strolling along air currents, needing barely a wing-beat to steady themselves. A heron glides past on deeply arched wings, husbanding the updraught off the slope; it descends to a sheltered inlet to hunt fish in the shallows. A single curlew probes the wrack farther on.

Mediterranean heath (*Erica erigena*) grows in profusion along the path and up the mountain slopes on both sides of the bay. The tallest western heather, its woody stems are strong enough to be used for making lobster pots; at this time of year it is coming into flower; some plants are a mass of delicate lilac blossoms tipped with dark magenta stamens at the mouth. I bend forward to smell another plant in flower – gorse – and even catch a whiff of its coconut musk.

We stop in the shelter of a birch to drink hot tea and eat a sandwich. The low sun warms us even as it is threatened by drifting cloud, while to the north another shower whitens the atmosphere. As it comes closer we watch the grain of falling hail drawn like a veil across the water, but it does not reach us.

On our way back, I notice the wooded southern corner overlooking Bellacragher Bay, crowded with Scots pine, ash and birch. If these plantings of pine are non-native, they still manage to evoke the great stands of Scots pine that used to cover north Mayo following the last Ice Age, before climate change and woodland clearance removed them. All that remains of these early generations of pine are the roots preserved everywhere deep in the peat.

12th February

In the evenings this week, the roads have been littered with the remains of frogs smashed by the wheels of cars. On mild, drizzling evenings they move in thousands towards pools where they spawn.

Our visitors from SE England are delighting in the fact that sunset here comes about half an hour later. We have pushed the boundary of daylight to about six o'clock, and the window is already light when I wake at 7:45.

13th February

Bun 'a Sáil. I met a sheepman and we chatted; he had binoculars, and was checking to see if any sick sheep had come down from the hill. He complained about hard weather. According to him: the man who found the Neolithic remains in the cave had been swimming in Loch Dubh under Bengorm when he saw a fox emerge from the hillside and wondered where the animal had come from: that led him to the cave, where human bones dated to c. 3600 BC were found.

He named the crag above us as Bun 'a Sáil; we shared more placenames lore – he confirmed several that I had on the map in my bag. The crag has balconies heavy with wood rush and deep heather. Water was dripping constantly from the saturated fleece of wood rush.

I walked across the bog towards this crag and climbed the steep ramp under the main face. A raven pair that had been quartering the face moved away, calling.

All the hills above about 400 metres with a clean covering of snow, which also lay lower down in sheltered places as I climbed.

There were sheep on the heights at Bun 'a Sáil, but there was one hoofprint that was bigger, deer-size, and farther up I found hare prints in clean, pure drifts, where my boots sank in to knee-height.

Threatening skies from Glennamong had cleared, there were views across Clew Bay, and white peaks: Birreencorragh, Nephin Beg, Corslieve, Coire an Earraigh. The top of Corslieve is flattened, like the shoulders and head of a frog looking away to the north. I was hoping to see Coiscéim, but Bengorm had hidden it, and Bengorm itself was in cloud. White peaks against blue sky are impressive, but are equally so against a setting of dark grey cloud.

I plod on to the ridge at about 400 metres. As I do, the snow gets deeper and drier; there's an Alpine purity to the scene. I'm amazed to see a chironomid fly just hatched.

Tracks across snow drifts. The tracks turned and ended on one drift; two metres away, several long strokes where wing primaries of a large bird had marked the snow. This hare may have been taken by a raven or an eagle or a great black-backed gull – how else could the track have disappeared?

Unveiling the Sun

At the top of the ridge, the view across Clew Bay was monochrome, a black and white affair: turtle-backed islands, glare of sun on sea, silver, smithy-hammered, dark veils of sleet and snow being drawn across grey water. I stood for much of this time intact – just a few brief visitations of dry, pecking hail bouncing off my jacket like beads of polystyrene. The cold was jaw-stiffening.

I followed my own boot marks to make my way back. When I reached Bun 'a Sáil, I paused under the big crag to eat a snack. Sounds of water trickling, dripping. No bird sounds, not even the usual wren. The rock face looks suitable for an eyrie, though there's no mention of an eagle that I have discovered.

The first, and only, passerine to greet me was a stonechat as I made my way back across the bog. That, and a snipe I had seen earlier.

14th February

I opened the door to go to the car and heard skylarks; then I saw four over Lavelle's field, at last.

By this afternoon, the top of Birreencorragh was a grainy white-grey hump; yesterday's splendour was already over following a night's rain.

16th February

Srahmore-Letterkeen. 1.30-3.00 p.m. Rain, cold. White patches still on Bengorm and Nephin Beg. Streams high. No sign of a passerine in the forestry. Several sheep carcasses recently dumped at the roadside near the numbered panorama photo, already extensively scavenged: a dismal sight, though it keeps hoodie and fox alive. The spot seems too cramped to tempt down a raven – or an eagle for that matter.

17th February

Murrevagh-Mulranny. You could say that today, unofficially, spring has arrived. Rain stopped and temperatures rose. Sun shone in the afternoon. Two skylarks at Murrevagh. Two great black-backs and hoodies on the carcass of a porpoise.

Most of the snow gone from Coscéim and Bengorm. Only the top of Nephin is still capped white.

At home this evening, robins and dunnock singing at dusk.

19th February

Gorteen Lough. I went out at 5.30, with an hour of light left. The lake very still; no swans. Small numbers of wildfowl. I came down to the gate in the reeds. Five herring gulls flew past, an adult and four juveniles.

The ground very wet and poached after all the bad weather. I thought there was a fish in the trench, but the ripples got bigger, and a moorhen swam past underwater, then resurfaced ten metres away, and called. A kestrel left the big roosting pines and flew west. Song thrushes were singing and a water rail called from the western end.

Woodpigeons clattered out of the trees as I went past.

It was just on woodcock hour as I climbed back up the hill and crossed the gate. The lake was very clear, marked by the passage of duck and moorhen.

As I came back along the hazel hedge, the field slope was a green baize being drained of its colour by blackness; a Wedgewood-blue sky formed a vault above it, with the thumbnail rim of a new moon. I had reached the bright road when a woodcock flew into Lavelle's field to feed.

A blackbird sang in a bush at the old gravel pit. 6.45 when I got home.

20th February

Gorteen Lough. I walked down from the Aghagowla side. Two hares popped over the ditch: one stopped among the rushes, sat there, then loped away. I admired the rich tawny hue through dark brown on his face.

Three whoopers were feeding in the reeds on the far side at the bottom of John's place.

I stood for about twenty minutes to see if any trout would move to a fly and saw none. A call from the brambles (old otter den) alerted me: there was a male stonechat, its head brownish rather than black, a juvenile, I thought. The bird yawned briefly; it was jaded from the winter routine and its lonely pursuit of insects through sedges and grasses.

February has now brought winter very far, such that it has no memory of the decline from which it comes. The whoopers probing the vegetation in the reeds are cut off from memories of last summer, and inklings of their future far to the north, in two months' time, on Iceland's Skjagafjorður. Thrushes may be trying their songs from three or four different quarters, but the tunes are frozen against the obduracy of winter, which now has more cold in store, on its way from the Russian land mass.

Sunlight surrounds the stonechat, lighting it all round its feathery edge with incandescence; the same gleam is in the seed tassels of phragmites. Coal tits call mechanically, like machines.

For a few hours a week ago, there was warmth and movement. These creatures might have heard the blurting chirble of a skylark flying over, but if they did, even if they were confounded by a sense of something extraordinary about to unfold, that short thrill has been forgotten again, reclaimed by cold and barrenness. No-one has seen the tiny fists of buds on the hawthorn, opening a slight chink of red in the brown twigs – so slight, that it might only be hope that finds it. Otherwise there would be nothing to see.

Cold, clear weather is forecast for several days right through until early March; nothing is going to happen yet, unless the higher, wider light of the sun signals the extraordinary change about to start, which will bring garlands of marsh marigold to these muddy margins, hatch swarms of chironomids for hungry fish, and draw flocks of sand martins to this brisk water.

23rd February

After lunch, Jess and I parked at Bourke's and turned left up the road to Slinaun. There's a nice stream to the left of the road and some hazel and birch woodland on either side. We passed a van and trailer with a whining dog inside, and a hundred yards farther on a small scatter of terriers came trotting towards us. A man with a shotgun surveyed the country from the top of a low boundary wall ahead. So, where we had come to find a patch of relict woodland – which the hazel and birch is – hunters had come in search of the fox. Four hundred years after the Elizabethans, we are still alert to threats from the wilderness. I said, truthfully, that we had not seen a fox at Lugnafahy for a long time. He answered that they come out at night after lambs.

The margin of the road is starting to green up with cow parsley, mont bretia and the larger leaf of cuckoo pint. Here and there the primrose is in flower. A mile of shallow glen running east from Slinaun was space itself; pure, remote space ready to be filled by meadow pipit song in a few weeks' time, but now quite silent. There are some fine old barns here, memorials of a time when this was not a suburb, as it is now, but its own centre, a place intimately known.

The stream was running fast below the road, angry, remorseful at last night's rain. The emerging shoots of honeysuckle like little green butterflies perched on the tips of twigs in the hedge.

Unveiling the Sun

24th February

I parked on the main road near Derrinumeera and walked down a side road towards Derryribbeen. The overcast day was darkening to rain. A couple of hundred yards along there was a gaunt, two-storey stone house with outhouses, and an old tractor parked in a hay shed. A hooded crow did turns in the air above the trees, calling, protesting vigorously, or maybe warning that this place was cursed. It did its job, and after taking a couple of photos I walked on, convinced that this was no place to linger.

25th February

This evening I thought I saw a bonfire on the eastern horizon at about 8:30, but when I took up the binoculars I saw that it was the top of the rising moon, still almost full. Two bushes were in front of it, starkly patterned nerve-endings against the pale orange rim of the moon. When I ran upstairs to get this in the telescope, the moon at a higher angle had cleared the horizon and was now a mottled, patched, roughish thing, with shimmering margins. Once or twice a bat flew across its face.

26th February

The battle rages around Kyiv.

Walked with Jess in Glen Hest. A few shafts of light on a breezy, overcast morning; the last stripes of snow on Birreen.

The light is back, even though the sky is overcast, and the leaves of honeysuckle are showing well.

27th February

When you walk past Malcolm Smith's place at Slinaun, there's a shallow valley to the north-east. The land is open pasture, neatly parcelled into fields by fence posts. At first you don't see the wire strung between, only the fence posts and the cream-coloured sheep. The posts inhabit the distance, giving it a graduated structure, a controlled perspective; curiously pleasing to know that people spent time out there, their heads swept by different weathers, shouting instructions at each other, swapping gossip, talking cattle, football, illness. The posts remember these ephemera, memorials to that time, graves of each moment.

28th February

Gorteen. I went down to the lake from the Aghagowla side. Water had frozen in the hoof marks; ice crunched under my boots. Two hares bounded away, white socks. A bullfinch called in the hedge, stayed among thorns and brambles as if captive in a cage. One branch of hawthorn has buds the size of grape seeds – this must have attracted the bullfinch.

When I crossed the fence into the rusty section just above the otter brambles, the whoopers saw me and stopped feeding; they swam in a group of five towards me, uttering their wheezy notes. I walked the shore among reeds looking for otter spraint: there was a black, tarry scat which I couldn't smell fish from, and lots of runs: mink or otter, I couldn't be sure. Farther along, at the second wood stump, I found a grey vomit-like spraint and this time it was essence of trout. Otter.

The whoopers, their necks richly stained with ochre, followed me like sentries; their acoustic insistence said that I did not belong there. I felt obscurely oppressed at having lost anonymity, become visible.

Crossed back into the rushes and went over the fence into the next field. Two more snipe – and a little jack – rose. The ground here was not fully frozen, allowing them a scant opportunity to forage. The jack snipe could have summered in Arctic Russia. It migrated many kilometres west to escape the Siberian cold.

Unveiling the Sun

A flock of lapwing crossed the sky, moving towards the coast for a chance of milder ground; a stonechat pair flicked and chatted along the fence between two long fields. The two hares ran off again, and bolted through the gate at the top, near the road.

Our feelings of spring are being flatly contradicted by Siberian cold; birds were struggling even before this extreme cold snap, now the weather hammers them even further and many small birds will die. Will we lose the stonechats again? They were decimated by cold winters seven or eight years ago and have only lately recovered. Despite all this, hawthorns show a few tiny greenish fists opening here and there, enough to feed a bullfinch.

At three in the afternoon, a freezing, obscuring dry-snow squall leaves a film of white on green.

March

1st March

The Beast from the East. Precipitation from Storm Emma will hit cold air from Siberia on Thursday. Met Éireann's red weather alert has been extended to the whole country. Ferries, buses and trains have mostly been cancelled. Schools in Leinster and Munster are shut today and tomorrow. All schools and third-level colleges are closed. People in the east and south of the country are being advised to stay at home from 16.00 today, Thursday, until lunchtime tomorrow. Over 400 flights in and out of Dublin airport were cancelled yesterday.

Snow has been reported from most of the country overnight, but Mayo has not had a lot. No snow fell here last night, and only light falls are forecast for tonight.

The news bulletins are full of reports from local correspondents: road closures, hospital staff staying in hotels to be sure of getting to work (Tullamore), gritters and salt spreaders working through the night, all but a handful of rough sleepers being brought in to emergency accommodation (a few refusing to go in: one man sleeping in a tent by the Grand Canal staying put). The negativity that dominates normal news coverage is replaced by national solidarity as the storm approaches this evening, though a lot of snow fell yesterday and in the east and south last night.

16:30 -1°C. Wind brisk from the east, no snow yet. 'Chonálfadh sé na corra – it would freeze the herons.' J.A. Baker describes such a bird, frozen where it stood in snow, 'in his thin sarcophagus of ice' – January 9th, *The Peregrine*.

The main weather event is forecast from now on, starting in the south as storm Emma arrives and hits cold air from the Siberian land mass.

17:00 Wrapped in waterproof leggings, in a face-freezing easterly wind, Jessica and I walked to Gorteen Lough. A flock of starlings, fieldfares [siocáin, from sioc, frost], and redwing on Lavelle's shoulder field; four lapwing rose from ground near the gate and flew down to the hollow with the feeders. Ravens called from the pines. Because the ground was frozen, the going was easier than before, when everything was wet.

Five whoopers on the lake, feeding in the reeds. Blasts of wind scudding grey on the water; a great black-back banking over the lake, heavy-winged, saying that there was carrion on this ground. Raven and great black-backs prosper in this kingdom of death; a raven did a roll above the oak grove this afternoon, exulting in this weather, to which many creatures succumb.

I walked a stretch of the bare slope, dropped down to the edge of the reeds to see if anything was stirring: a few teal and mallard took off from the stream.

A scatter of feathers by the hedge, a sparrowhawk kill.

Everything thin and sere under the oaks.

MARCH

2nd March

This late-winter weather event from Siberia combines with geo-political unease about Russian belligerence in Syria and Ukraine, and meddling in elections in the west.

At the same time, scientists are alarmed by 'crazy' temperature rises in the Arctic. 'An alarming heatwave in the sunless winter Arctic is causing blizzards in Europe'. Global warming is said to be eroding the polar vortex, the powerful winds that once insulated the frozen north. In this hypothesis, the polar vortex becomes less stable, sucking in more warm air and expelling more cold fronts, such as those currently being experienced in the UK and northern Europe.

Weather as geo-politics, driven by our own profligacy. Anthropocene weather.

A couple of centimetres of dry, powdery snow; it had blown off the drive and drifted at the front door. A pied wagtail enquired at the door forlornly and left the design of its feet.

Most of the snow was in the east and south of the country; Mayo got a relatively small amount.

Jessica and I went out to Gorteen Lough, calling first to see John's lambs, small sets of twins and triplets curled up on straw under lamps, or suckling persistently. We chatted to young Louis, who wisely insists that 'there's no money in sheep farming'; their work is sustained by loyalty to the home place.

John has built several nursery pens in the big shed and has about thirty lambs born, but as more come, he will be in difficulty if the cold weather persists and he is not able to put them out. Young lambs would perish if left out in this weather.

We carried on and climbed to the top of the drumlin, into the cold breeze. A couple of ravens were gliding above the whaleback, well fed on sheep carrion in this weather. A couple of lapwing squealed and rose from the top. Jessica gasped at the bleak splendour of the view to the north and stopped to take pictures. The five whoopers were still there on the far side and launched into the water when they saw us.

On our way down to the bottom of John's place, there were hare prints in drifted snow along the gorse hedge, and tridents of crows and ravens that had foraged there earlier. We tried sitting on the old waxed Burberry as a makeshift toboggan to get us down. Lapwing took off from the slope, with a golden plover among them.

We met the lapwing again at the top gate on our way out – like portions of a dressmaker's fabric, felt-like and rounded, they corkscrewed away over the horizon.

Less cold than yesterday, the snow thawing gradually.

Wind-noise in the chimney this evening.

3rd March

Snow overnight. Not the dry, powdery, flyaway snow of Emma, but the usual wet variety that thaws quickly. Photos from Kildare show snowdrifts covering cars.

Jessica and I walked through the oak grove into the field. There are snow-free patches near the gate where sheep slept overnight. Their fleece is a warm yellowish tone beside the abstraction of snow. A few larks and pipits are at the hay feeder where the ground is exposed from trampling. The larks must have fled from the east, where they normally stay in winter.

We crossed the field to the river, following the larks. The Moyour flowing very clear and pure, the same element as the snow lying all around. In the concentration of light, under a grey sky, the rippled pattern of sediment on the river bed was very clear. A long bank of a very thin water weed undulated steadily in a shallow flow, with a great intensity of green.

At the western end, where snow has collected into an

eighteen-inch drift, the prints of a hare: the animal had come through the fence and loped up along the drift, it must have enjoyed the pure depth of virgin snow as much as we do.

Five lapwing flew across and landed in the field, close to heaps of sheep manure – nothing to feed on there; these birds must be close to starvation. Jessica thinks that lapwing are like a child's image of a bird.

Snow reflects so much light, giving an unusual intensity to colour. I marvel again at the vividness of paintings and drawings in the house.

4th March

Hawthorn starting to bud. Saw the male thrush on a cable briefly. He was in the full flush of sexual excitement, his head feathers ruffled up and his mandibles apart. He looked deranged.

Finished my translation of this poem:

The Great Eagle
from the Irish of Féilim Mac Dhúill

1
I got up in a rage on Sunday morning,
I put on my shoes and set out for Tír an Fhia.
On my way through Dead Man's Valley there was the Great Eagle,
Like a small rick of turf he was, lording it in his station.
I called him a waster, a layabout, an idiot, a fool,
Like Brian Mac Lóbais from the seed of Cathal Buí,
And seven curses on top of that all over him forever
For taking my fine young cock, who used to call to me.

2
"Can you come to your senses and not be insulting me like that;
I can assure you on my honour, I wouldn't take this to court;
And I don't think you'd have much to gain in your own situation,
Because you're a man who was always generous to the traveller.
Turn back now, go home and yourself ask Nora
For the name of the young woman who was wrecking her head.
There was some amount of feathers all over their laps in the kitchen;
They had a feast between them and not one of them was grateful."

3
You're lying, you robber, they wouldn't eat it together,
Or anything else like it, without the word getting out.
But you were the one who snatched it under your big wings,
And the autumn season won't be over before I get you to court.
I have a share of books of ancient history stored in my cupboard;
Your father was one of the greatest rogues in the country,
You'd find the widow's hen in his nest late in the day,
That and every other kind of mischief you could count.

4
"As long as the Fianna were alive in my time I was a fine young lad,
I wasn't trained in thieving but I always spread enchantment,
With fine games and exploits, scaling peaks and combat,
Until I was left in this predicament, a painful case!
And there are more stories that I've not told you yet."
As if he heard their voices, his eyes filled with tears:
"The legends will tell you I'm a son of Red the Great,
And if you're looking for a fight, stand and face me. You'll be sorry."

5
He got decked out in his finery, his weapons and his armour,
The sword he had was the sharpest you could find,
Me with my spade and no protection but my shirt,
So we ran at each other very early in the day.
You'd see the sparks flying from the clash of our weapons,
And half an hour before the sun went down he had to call a truce;
We were like two bulls locked in combat in a mountain valley,
And neither of us had a clue who was the better man.

6
He sent me written notice on the day after that,
That we would fight for certain the following morning.
But may Donnelly bestow grace, if he lived in this area
He'd give me satisfaction or he'd die trying.
The answer I sent him was that I never shook with fear
Before any man who landed with courage from the sea.
I got up in the morning and made light work of the journey
And now you're going to hear how I came out on top.

7
Neighbour, do you appreciate the victory won by Féilim
When he overcame that mindless brute with a fierce reputation?
He went head to head with a giant bigger than Howth Head,
Or did you think at all that I'd get out of there alive?
The first blow I landed, I struck a bone to floor him;
He fell and I can say my own head was in a spin.
"Leave off now and don't kill me, and I'll praise you forever;
You defended Ireland's honour without thought of reward."

    This poem is a rare example of an eagle in Irish literary tradition which is founded on an experience of the depredations of a wild bird, and not on the eagle as a conventional emblem of power, as it is in heraldry.

The poet Féilim Mac Dhúill was a mill owner from the Tír an Fhia area of south Connemara. His dispute with the eagle arose when his wife accused the eagle of carrying off a favourite bird of Féilim's, which used to wake the poet every morning; he sets out to find the eagle and confront him; the ensuing dialogue is peppered with references to litigation, as the poet tries to get satisfaction for his loss. The eagle speaks to him and says that his wife killed the cock to cook it for a woman who was visiting. This humanised eagle, far from being a creature of strength, is a damaged figure: he says that he used to be a member of the heroic Fianna until the modern world reduced him to snatching poultry from people's yards. He still puts on his armour and takes up weapons for the ensuing fight, where he is eventually defeated.

This poem, which travelled throughout Connemara and was later recorded from the Joyce Country, contains a few obscurities from being transmitted orally, but the figure of the eagle is a superb case of how the wild was understood in the folk tradition as a degenerated state, a corruption of some former state of heroism and nobility. This contempt for large raptors in the wild is still a strong reflex among country people, and it still works against the acceptance of these birds in some areas following reintroductions.

5th March

The fields around us are free of snow and frost, but the mountains on the horizon are white. The Sheeffry Hills are draped in white, as if set to stage the story of Shackleton's adventure.

On our walk today we saw the first coltsfoot in flower near the cemetery. A treecreeper beyond Niland's. The whooper swans have now gone from Clogher, and from Gorteen.

MARCH

6th March

The Reek still white, like a cone of newly sifted flour.

9th March

Calm, mild and overcast; everything starting to bud now, pond-skaters on a stream and even a cranefly in flight. A skylark and a meadow pipit in song at Kiltyroe. The Owennabrockagh, downstream of Brockagh Bridge, is a wonderful, lively, rushing stream over dark stones. Alders and ash line its course so that the river is a band of woodland, with another shining fleeing element at its base; after a kilometre the river runs into a dull channel flowing obediently among the fields. The next bridge downstream from Brockagh Bridge is a superb single limestone arch. Otters have been there, as I saw from spraint on the sill at the base. I ended my walk at Kiltyroe when I came to the saddle and heard the sound of another river, the Rossow, below me; I had reached the watershed between two catchments so I turned back, as if the Owennabrockagh were my territory and I had no business farther on.

12th March

Diarmaid came to rehearse for Tuesday's reading – a violent wind got up as we practised. A raven swooped down into the garden to pick up a stick for a nest.

13th March

This morning I cut and dug out some more rushes from the corner of the garden with the billhook and the shears. The American alder beside me is just beginning to sprout leaves the size of the tip of a cotton bud.

In the afternoon I went to the lake to fish, but the day seemed too cold for any prospect of feeding trout. The field I crossed had not been entered since I visited about a fortnight ago, and the spring seemed slow, reluctant. A flock of eleven lapwing – the biggest I have seen here – took off from O'Donnell's side and flew away to the west. A mechanical digger clearing some old ditches on the horizon above the lake was a sound I am unaccustomed to in this secluded, rather lonely place.

After ten minutes' fishing I rose one hefty trout and then hooked a fish, probably the same one, a couple of yards nearby. It escaped, but it was heartening to know that something was inclined to move at this early date in the angler's calendar. At my feet I could see small flies on the water: Michael Kingdon calls these reed smuts and is exercised by the challenge of imitating them with an artificial fly. They are, he says, an early food supply for trout tempted up from the morose depths of winter.

One trout was all that appeared. The marsh marigold is well advanced. In a brief spell of sunlight a skylark took off from the field behind me and pitched up to sing – an Apollonian harp. As I came away a raven flew out from one of the pines at the eastern end of the lake: so that's where the ravens breed. As I drove back I saw Nephin with a dusting of snow; no wonder the day felt too cold, and a wonder that any trout should be inclined to take. As they say in Mayo, nuair a bhíonn sneachta ar Néifinn bíonn sé fuar in Éirinn.

I pass a girl in army uniform walking the road on my way home.

15th March

I walked out in the afternoon through Gorteen and Derrynaraw and then back to Brockagh. A kestrel flew past at Derrynaraw, very thin in aspect, enough to hold perception for a few moments, a shard of power holding out among the crows in crow country.

The river has fallen back after all the floods. I looked down from the big single-arched bridge and a vividly yellow frog plopped into the water – it had been sunning itself on the bank before I appeared. It swam across the river, a naked little man with narrow hips.

The wood beyond the house among the birches tempted me in. Down by the river I found some early wood anemones and noticed shoots of bluebells on the way. Lovely seclusion, shelter, and a shrine-like stillness. More old otter spraint on a high rock that had not been washed over by floods. There is more hazel woodland on the other side, and I thought of the wonder that this place will become when the leaves are out and the blackcap has arrived. No grazing animals, thankfully. A little stream, a tiny thing, meanders and murmurs down through this woodland, enough to attract kids to build small dams and make little mill wheels from sticks and leaves.

As I approached Brockagh from the west, the tall poles of birches were swaying like the masts of yachts being rocked by a gale.

16th March

Drizzling, not mild, at the lake. A pair of whoopers, their calls were like a faulty bellows that March was working but not managing to get any warmth from the fire of spring.

17th March

At last, some good fishing: the day was blustery, from the west, and there was nothing doing at the eastern end of the lake with choppy water rushing towards me and the wind slapping my fly line back at me. But the day was mild, so I tried some of the sheltered spots along the northern margin, and, sure enough, I started to meet trout. They all took the dropper fly: a scruffy little thing with a black body and some badgery hackle. I don't know what it's called. There were trout rising – for reed smuts I suppose – and they came readily to my fly. I caught about seven, and kept two. They weighed 1lb 5ozs together. None of the smaller trout were showing yet. All of these fish were at or over half a pound. No sea trout, though. If there were any this winter, the big flood in January may have taken them back to sea.

A big grey sparrowhawk swooped over the reeds above me.

18th March

Went back to Ciarán's for a cup of tea. He quizzed me about Gorteen Lough. Told me that people wondered who the man with binoculars was. He lent me the Fahy handbook. My walks have made people nervous, they are afraid of break-ins.

19th March

Blowing a gale here this morning – taking last year's leaves off the oaks.

22nd March

Fished at Delphi with Chris Huxley and Digby Lewis. Chris got a 9lb wild fish at Waterfall Pool, which I landed and released. There were kelts in Turn Pool, and a few fish in the river. Plenty of salmon and kelts in Fin Lough, which we fished to no avail in the morning.

29th March

Down to the lake in the evening. Not a puff of wind at first, but then rain moved in and fell steadily for about an hour in virtual calm. As I tackled up I heard a single golden plover call; it expressed all the loneliness of the uplands. The rain was an infinite series of detonations across the surface of the lake. A few trout took, all but one wriggled off.

As the rain eased, the drains were full of muddy water: one was like the hill at Joyce's side squatting down on her hunkers to discharge into the lake. Silt spread into the lake at that point: a tiny delta. At the eastern end, the slow trench draining into the lake could be heard as a bright sound of running water. It ran muddy and strong, seven or eight feet wide, full of twigs and bits of torn-up plants, streaming over the reedmace and phragmites to get to the lake. A stream like this must push enough silt into the lake to provide spawning beds for fish; the famous sea trout would be tempted into a stream like this too. The new shoots of yellow iris are about six inches high, like green flames. Marsh marigold in bloom.

As I left, something swam across the perfectly calm lake (mink, rat, or moorhen?) leaving a silver trail as purposeful and direct as the vapour of a plane.

31st March

At Glennamong, watching the breezes gathering at the river mouth and scudding across the lake. The wind makes dark marks, like iron filings being marshalled by magnetism, then these intensify and spread, until a vast multitude, merged into one epic army, are swept over the water, as if running towards one of the great battles of antiquity.

April

1st April

Jessica announced that there was 'a swan on the lawn', and fooled me. Later, I thought I saw a bird flashing past, low over the ground, whereas it was the shadow of a passing crow – fooled again.

2nd April

In the hazy sunlight of early morning, two cock pheasants squared up to each other in Martin's field next door – a ritual territorial joust. One eventually flew away into Lavelle's across the road. The birds' colours were exotic, brilliant, in low sunlight.

6th April

A pair of great black-backed gulls on the big field, like monuments. I saw them scavenging a lamb carcass. They wash in the puddles of lying water, preen, and sit.

7th April

Walked a section of the Castlebar-Newport road east of Derrinumeera (where all the bog deal is on the surface) to see a tributary of the Owennabrockagh that runs down from the forestry at Lappallagh. A nice little stream running under the road, through the drum of a bridge that has lost the top of its parapet into the river. As I walked on, I met the Owennabrockagh again where it joins the main road – a 'developer' has straightened its course here, turning it into a naked canal for a stretch; a row of hawthorns has been cut with a chainsaw, with foot-high stumps left along the river, like moorings on a wharf. A stonechat pair here. A trout rose under the culvert.

I turned right off the main road and walked back through Derrintloura: on the good farm that you pass near the T junction, a single beech (the planter's tree) on its own, in the attitude of a tree that has been exposed to the west winds. A squall came on as I walked. At Ass Bridge, an old man walking; he was in his dotage and did not engage with me. The wood anemones at Brockagh are very beautiful, in splendid order.

11th April

Fine, mild day at Srahduggaun. Walked a transect for Cameron over the bog, to mark grouse droppings, etc. Rose one grouse. Saw extensive otter tracks through the bog, running from one lochán to another. Lizards here and there on tussocks sunning themselves. My companion and I saw three in one kilometre.

13th April

Fished the lower Sheean beat with Chris. River very high. We tackled up and walked down, Chris got as far as the junction. I saw one fish turn in Red Pool, Chris saw one in Junction Pool.

Unveiling the Sun

No take. A beautiful spring day, meadow pipits pairing up and singing. A peregrine swung down briefly after a mallard but gave up and flew back towards Slieve Alp. I heard a golden plover on the moor near Lagduff.

Weary from tramping, I stared at a blackface sheep. The animal was curious about me; as I stared at it, it gradually grew more self-conscious, like a woman extravagantly dressed in a massive fur coat, who is made nervous by her own ostentatiousness. I saw how superbly kitted these animals are for the bitter conditions on these moors.

16th April

At the outflow of the Newport River from Lough Beltra. Heard the cuckoo for the first time this year. The sky full of larks and meadow pipits. I meant to walk to Drumilra (eagle ridge), but I got distracted by the lake, as is often the case.

17th April

Returning from a walk three days ago, we found a rabbit on the road, recently killed. The body was virtually unmarked. It had started to rain a few minutes earlier. I removed the body to the verge. The dry patch of road under the body formed a perfect rabbit shape, with a small dribble of blood at the snout.

I went to a piece of woodland near Josie Cusack's house to listen for a blackcap – heard two, and saw a beautiful display of wood anemones.

18th April

A big apricot moon this evening.

19th April

On the Rock House beat of the Owenduff. I fished down the way, saw nothing.

As the river falls, and with it any real chance of a fish, and with sun on the river, you curse everything about the place: the sun, the peat, the rhododendrons, your own impulsiveness at having come here at all and paid money for the experience. All this on an evening when the rest of the world is sitting at a pub window or even on a pub terrace, thinking how beautiful the day is, how the weather has come good at last.

20th April

Our swallows arrived in the porch today. Very mild, but hazy, overcast.

21st April

Afternoon walk to Drumilra with Jess. Bright, breezy; some sausage-machined peat newly cut on the bog. Peacock butterflies.

24th April

Stopped at the level crossing near Islandeady when I heard a blackcap close by, and saw him, in the top branches of a – still bare – ash tree, singing vigorously. He was the colour of the ash branches, and from where I watched below him I could not see his black cap. His song was as full as the song thrush, but like a jazz improvisation on the same theme.

28th April

Jessica happened to say that we had not seen a fox for a long time: two hours later, as if to oblige, a fox appeared in the field below us, trotting towards the carcass of a lamb. I had noticed hoodies poking at its rear end, but it was still virtually intact when the fox arrived. A couple of lambs thought briefly about confronting this strange new red-and-muddy-coloured thing starting to tear at their dead sibling, but backed off when the fox stiffened and they soon lost interest. The fox, a female, tore into the lamb at the hindquarters, opening up the stomach, and eventually separating a hind leg. It ran off towards the ditch with this trophy and we watched it through a telescope as, partly hidden by rushes, it went to work.

Hoodies and one or two magpies hung around meanwhile, but they scattered when the fox came back to pull at the lamb's insides. The fox took a mouthful of something from the lamb and again set off with it, but this time it paused twenty metres away, pushed open a hollow in the ground, and stuffed this parcel of offal into it. (Lynda tells me that lions in Africa do the same thing with the intestinal parts of their carrion, to get rid of parts they consider vile.) Again the fox returned to the carcass, ate some more, and eventually stopped to lick its paws. Through the telescope I could see its yellow eyes.

Then a raven arrived, mobbed by two hoodies. We discovered that the raven gives way to the fox, so the hierarchy at the carrion is: fox, raven, hoodie, magpie. The raven flew off to the ditch and promptly found the severed shank left by the fox, so it had its portion.

The vixen presumably had decided that her best chance of a meal was during daylight: at night the bully boys would be out and she'd have little chance in the tussle. Her flabby tummy suggested that she had recently whelped, so she may have been very hungry and was searching for food for her cubs.

A fox's brush is like a guilty ghost of itself, tagging along behind it.

29th April

Yesterday's fox put in an appearance again today, passing down through the field next to the house. The whimbrel have arrived.

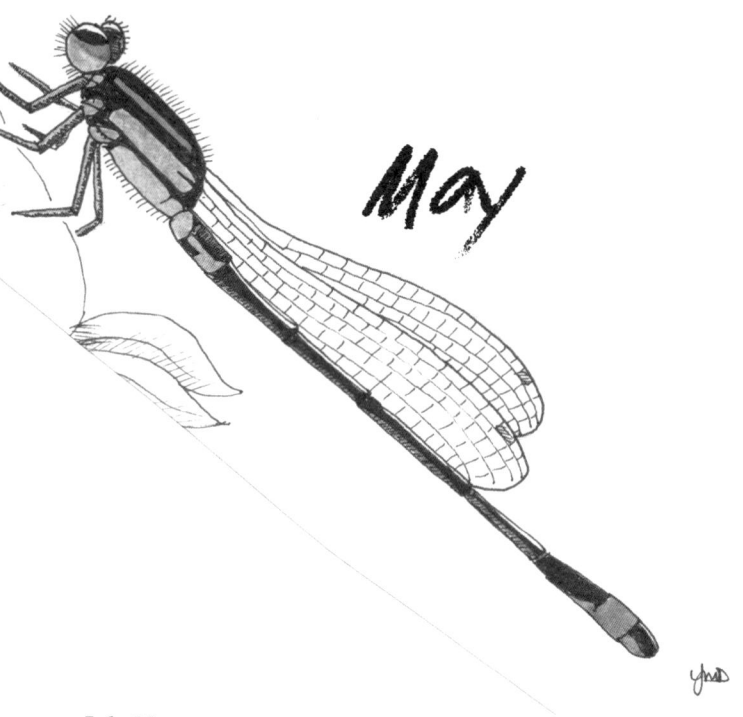

5th May

At Rock House with Jess, Chris, Lynda, Digby and Alison.

The drought broke on Saturday night, and this morning I was woken by a gentle caress of sound on the roof of the bedroom: rain, rain for the fisherman.

The camellias and rhododendrons are spectacular, vivid and intense; the entire woodland is carpeted with three-cornered leek – looks superficially like a 'white' bluebell. The groundsman Johnny is busy about the place with his mower and his pack of setters and spaniels.

The gauge in the side stream was at 9 when we arrived. A gale blowing down the river, strong from the south, very mild. The river high, and still rising. Debris of rushes and rhododendron. Later, when I saw Chris down the river ahead of me, I thought that a salmon angler in these conditions looked like a Yeti absorbed in some forlorn science, measuring river flow with repeated draughts of a line, as if fly-fishing had nothing to do with catching fish.

The common sandpiper, sentry of the shingle, was well established, pairs banking and dashing up and down, or settled on a rock, posing with the elements.

The points of yellow of the gorse flowers a peppering of colour above the dull-orange rock. Punk ridge-hair of faded, colourless rushes; some large chunks of peat falling away from a bank on the far side. Once, fishing, I was startled by a form suddenly turning and rising in the water, spring salmon, or otter – no! A chunk of peat, then another one, rolling along the shallows. The river here does a great omega, the neck getting narrower, liable to break through fairly soon.

17.00-19.00. Returned to the river in the afternoon. River still rising, still coloured. None of us saw anything. Wind had dropped.

In the evening, around the fire, Alison played an app with bird calls on her iPad, including golden plover calls, which had haunted me when I heard them at night last winter.

6th May

Rock House. Wine has not agreed with me; I spent part of the night tossing and turning, but I'm enjoying the sound of 'soft' rain sweeping across the roof above the bedroom, keeping the river topped up. The setters are wandering through the garden, and their barks echo in the high vaults of the ancient conifers.

Fished downstream from Blue Lodge. Chris had a six-and-a-half-pound fish from High Bank Pool on his favourite fly, a Baldrick. As we sat in the lodge at lunchtime the rain set in. Conditions had been ideal in the morning. Several common sandpipers. Conversation at lunch centred on mortality. Digby is a cancer survivor. I suggested that I'd rather die by the river from a heart attack than spend fifteen years in a nursing home.

Unveiling the Sun

I watched Digby tying double Baldricks by the window at Rock House (at about 17.00). The Baldrick and the Lord Lewis are patterns we favour when fishing the Owenduff. The hooks Digby was using were Limerick hooks, size 6. 'Limerick' refers to the shape of the hook, with a sharply angled bend. Having tied the body and the tail, and allowing them to set, Digby then took a bunch of mixed bear and squirrel hair and tied it to the head of the hook, tied black thread to the head, and finished with nail varnish to bind it. He worked at the vice, like Krapp under his lamp, who felt 'less alone'.

Much conversation about the psychology of spring salmon fishing, the necessity of self-belief, concentration, tenacity. Digby and I need to believe in the prospect of a salmon. Fish being caught at Lagduff (three), Sheean (one) and our (Chris's) fish at Rock House.

Walked in the woods at Rock House: bugle in bloom, streams and little channels running full; rhododendrons and azaleas in great array; camellias slightly over; everything very damp; old firs and pines in decline.

7th May

Rock House. Light rain this morning.

High water, falling throughout the day in overcast conditions.

Digby: 11lb+ from High Bank

SL: 5½lb from Otter Pool

CH: 5lb from the flats upstream from High Bank

LH: 7½lb (Lynda was away most of the day and fished High Bank for 35 minutes only)

Four anglers, four fish; SL struck another in Beach Pool briefly.

A common sandpiper nest with four eggs on the shingle near

Round Pool. The bird flew off, fluttering like a wind-up flying toy that cannot take off; it flapped violently on the stones to distract my attention; I marked the spot with a rotten fence post. I have found three common sandpiper nests in very different locations:

Nest 1, Tarsaghaun: grassy

Nest 2, Corry Lough: exposed peat, exposed location

Nest 3, on shingle near Black Banks

That evening, after champagne and dinner, animated and sometimes heated debate about killing salmon or releasing them. I was in a rage about the numbers of salmon and sea trout being taken from the Moy near Ballina. Chris and Lynda were insisting that they would not fish for sport only, but that they want to kill and eat their catch. (Sibylle intimated that she would prefer people to put back the fish.) My desire to kill salmon is waning, but not my desire to fish. The plan to walk to Corry Lough is looking unlikely as the day is overcast, with high winds forecast for the afternoon.

8th May

Rock House. Fished 10:30 to 12:15, gauge at 5, river dropping. I met Alan Cusack, the water keeper, who says fish in the upper reaches drop back after the flood. Lynda and I went up to Whinney, nothing. I noticed a pocket above Car Pool which I christened Jessica's.

The day drying up, with some brightness in the west. Lots of bluebells among the emerging stalks of bracken. We saw a pale mauve form of milkwort.

9th May

A bright, warm day. The hawthorn blossoms are in their buds but have not appeared yet. The hawthorn fly or bibbio hatched today in considerable numbers around the alders at the corner of the house and provided good sport for swallows. A whitethroat sang along the hawthorn hedge and from the electricity cable overhead. Marsh marigold in prime condition down at the lake. We checked the trap again for mink; still nothing caught after four days. Whimbrel appear to have moved on now.

11th May

We took up the mink trap as we had caught nothing.

12th May

A whitethroat has been singing around the house for a few days. He seems to like the setting, especially the overgrown hedge near the compost heap. We are delighted with the new visitor and want him to stay.

13th May

Went to the lake in the evening, just before dusk. A slight wind dropping away as I arrived at the shore. Heard whimbrel on the far side. Fished wet fly, but conditions too calm; switched to nymph and got a trout on a dropper, the 'fly' scarcely more than a hook with one winding of brown thread.

The new house on the drumlin a single beacon over the twilit lake – intrusive, but I'm sure they're watching TV, not me with my headlight, my cyclops beam taking me back among the yellow flag. Marigolds still splendid, though many flowers gone to seed now. A commotion in the reeds as I leave, perhaps a mallard family that has escaped the mink. The night totally calm. Rain begins as I write this at midnight.

14th May

I have read a lot of Beckett this year on the occasion of the centenary. Very rewarding, but I can't accept Beckett's dismissal of the natural world. For a while, Molloy recognises his part in the process of seasons, the dynamic of nature, then he returns to 'his jar', 'which knew neither seasons nor gardens.' In *Endgame*, Clov declares that 'there's no more nature'.

One thing, though: *The Unnameable* identifies how nature has been understood in visual terms, sometimes to the exclusion of the other senses. 'But the eye, let's leave him his eye too, it's to see with, this great wild black and white eye, moist, it's to weep with, it's to practise with, before he goes to Killarney.'

15th May

The lake was a grey cauldron at dusk, the water warm in the rain. As I came away, the grass among the rushes was like a frail moss or something insubstantial, gloomy. A few lady's smock are showing here and there among dark clumps of rushes, a barely perceptible pink in the dusk, the only flower in a green gloaming. Grey cloud slips ever lower over the horizon as I get back to the car, a narrow hearse awaiting its driver. Sheep still at their miserable business of foraging, like the souls of the dead who have not yet managed to cross the Styx.

17th May

With Mark Wormald. We drove to Tubbrid and parked at Ray's house, Mark marvelling at the scenery. Got the rods out and marched purposefully to Loch Geal. We walked around to the outflow, a narrow little stream perhaps nine or ten inches deep, not much more than a foot across, going into a hollow filled with molinia tussocks, almost disappearing. We thought there was enough there for a sea trout to pass.

The lake is low, an exposed margin of stones. A cormorant was perched on a rock and took off as we emerged from the tree-cover: a sign of fish. We started to fish on the western shore. Mark saw a big fish – a few pounds he reckoned – turn and surge on the surface; we watched some movement in the bay near the outflow. Nothing took, not when we moved to the eastern shore either. The lake edge is shallow, rocky or sandy; only in one stretch of the eastern shore did I find a depth of water (four feet plus) within sight of my boots. Mark's report of a big fish way out was tantalising, but it was strange that nothing came to the fly. There was enough wind to keep a jabble on the water. We thought that fish might avoid the shallows until late in the day.

We walked on to Loch na mBreac, less than a kilometre away.

Mark fished from the southern shore, with wet flies; I fished from the opposite side. A few fish rose to me and I landed two, small four-to-five-ounce brownies, the dark colour you'd expect; then a trout that fought harder, a silver sea trout, about four ounces, looking famished, but very bright in the flanks.

The outflow stream is more rapid and fuller, gurgling over stones right at the edge of the lake, then becoming dark and peaty as it runs parallel to the track before entering a culvert. On Barry Dalby's map it is named Muingwee, the yellow swamp, because of the tussocks of molinia in the hollow where it leaves the lake. This is a more substantial stream than the one out of Loch Geal: both flow into the Altnabrocky River.

Mark had a couple of brownies from his side, both small, and lost a bigger fish.

We snacked on cake and coffee, then marched out. Bog bean starting to flower in a boggy, flooded depression beside the road.

A mallard and two ducklings – the mother did an elaborate injury-feigning, tottering down the track like an aircraft with collapsed wings, to distract us from her young.

Many signs of deer around the lakes and along the tracks; not a single bootmark anywhere away from the track. We neither saw nor heard anyone else all day.

18th May

I sat in the garden between the two hazels and realised that a robin pair were feeding young in a nest on the ground just beside Blackbird Alley. They hesitated a lot before going in because I was there. Jessica arrived, and we watched them. They were still very hesitant. Then Jessica decided to go back to the house, and when she did, the robins returned immediately and were less shy than before. They scarcely noticed me: they thought 'the human' had gone back to the house with Jessica, and I remained as a natural part of the garden. All this is going on ten yards from the kitchen window but it was only revealed when I sat in the garden, taking a different perspective.

19th May

Just off the train from Dublin after an afternoon spent watching masses of growth everywhere. Hawthorn with may blossom especially magnificent. I had to go to the lake for a while, but rain came in just as I was setting out. I nonetheless went down, the rain having reduced the lake to a grey, featureless surface: the odd swirl of a feeding trout. I fished through the rain; the lake was very high so I could not wade in on the southern side and had to go round instead, trudging through heavy, new growth. The irises will be out in a few days – a few flower heads about to unfold. You hate the lake on a day like this, and you hate the mindless sheep that fill every crevice with the stink of their piss. Even your boots stink of sheep piss when you arrive home. This evening I noticed a few leaves of wood sorrel appearing under the old oak at the top of the slope, and some butterwort in flower. Not enough to redeem the misery of a wet evening. The possibility of sea trout in this lake takes me out on an evening like this. One fish snapped at the little teal-blue-and-silver on my dropper and broke the dropper off. Sin an méid a bhí. By the time this is written the rain has abated, just to tantalise. Hugh Falkus was right: fishing is little good in rain.

20th May

Grey, breezy weather postpones the summer again. This morning I watched the leaves of the trees being blown about by the kind of wind that rises ahead of a shower. No sign of the swallows. In fact, there was nothing in the picture that gave any suggestion of vitality. Very little beyond waiting, the boredom of a summer continually deferred.

I've done enough fishing on lakes so far. I feel the need to get away from the grey surface of lakes to a river, and a body of water that is constantly flowing, shifting, adapting.

21st May

Met John Quinn in Newport, a man with a flamboyant Victorian moustache who has his shed near the river. He spotted me admiring his plantings of cabbage and tree seedlings. At once he offered me a box of oak seedlings, for nothing. He recommended putting acorns in a bucket of water, to test them. The ones that float can be rejected. You should put the good ones in the fridge, and within a couple of weeks they begin to germinate. Alders were the fastest to grow: 'They'd grow in a spit,' he said.

When I asked him if they were getting any salmon on the Newport River he was dismissive, but the place was 'black' with smolts on their way back to the sea.

I had to defer his offer of trees until I decided where I would put them. When I arrived back home, I noticed that our neighbours had cut down all their trees on the westerly side, just as we struggle to establish our plantings on that side.

23rd May

Nephin Forest. Chatted to Ray, from Dublin, who lives at the end of the road at Tubbrid. Floundered through tussocks past the boggy mire of the first lake to Lough Keeran. The lake appears as a sudden floor of shimmer under the lodgepoles. Relied on my map. Water beetles scudding across the surface, no rising fish. Signs of deer. Lots of damselflies and dragonflies patrolling the mossy, heathery margins.

Hard, dry 'chup' of crossbills, sighing calls of siskins, robin song, coal tit and chaffinch calls. A common sandpiper on the lake. Enough breeze to keep down the midges. I eat a sandwich at the outflow and carry on to today's prize: Lough Doo. Both lakes drain into the Altnabrocky system.

As I arrive at Lough Doo, the flowers on the lodgepoles disperse pollen in generous puffs as I pass. I fish on the northern shore – nothing, then I move and hear the gurgling of a stream entering the lake, a happy sound of life and connection to relieve the inertia of the bog. Sandpipers here are very active and vocal, one bird flying high in territorial display above the trees, like a wader of the taiga, gliding back and forth, appearing at moments like a swift. I walk round in drifts of dragonflies and damselflies and fish again in the peaty depth – nothing. A sandpiper flies out silently from the heathery fringe at my feet; the nest must be on a ledge in the peat just over the water.

From Lough Doo I make it back to the track through a clearing in larch, past a lochán full of sphagnum. Then I strike out for the track, which takes longer to reach than expected. When I eventually get to a grassy, lit clearing, the track is higher up, totally colonised by lanky lodgepole pines, growing skinny in the shade cast by older trees. I rarely cross the forest off-piste, so it is a relief to be on firm footing after a long time spent on tussocks of heather and sphagnum.

Back at Loch na mBreac, it's too bright for my liking, but

there's enough breeze. On the southern side I catch two trout, one brown, one sea. I take a few scales from the sea trout and toss it back into the water. Satisfied with this piece of citizen science, I walk back out. There are several pine marten scats on the track; a large group of crossbills settles on pines close to a boggy lochán, calling; I saw one female up close, green in the late afternoon sun. Their calls were in the air most of the afternoon.

24th May

I drove to look at the Owennabrockagh near Josie Cusack's house. Still plenty of water, a full body of a stream: the irises around his well soon to flower. Golden-coloured olives buoyant, abundant below the bridge. As the car rounded a corner on a sheltered bend, flies in swarms appeared in the low, oblique light of the evening sun, each one a bearer of reflected sunlight, giving volume to space.

25th May

Re-reading Mark Wormald's book, *The Catch*: delighted at his way of following, retracing the stages of his research. The surprises, puzzles and satisfactions of making connections, juggling different elements of his project: his own memoir, Ted Hughes' life, the discovery of angling as a driver within Ted's life, his own angling trips to Ted's favourite places, the interpretation of poems, placing them in the context of places he loved, the rivers and lakes…

Barrie Cooke found Ted's intensity 'literally frightening'. 'He is quite dedicated to extracting everything out of himself and that doesn't just mean ART… He is more ruthless than me by far and that I find terribly admirable.'

'Barrie was electrified by Ted's visit… His visit had left him excited, invigorated, confirmed.' I could say the same about

Mark's visit: we too have a lot in common, I too feel 'invigorated' and 'confirmed' by his visit. He encourages me to forge ahead with the sea trout study; I see it as opening up a new window on the Nephins. Also: I could extract more from myself than just fishing, but I should follow the fishing, keep my eyes fixed on the fish, like the tip of the float that Ted had in mind as he spoke to the children about thought, the connection with things that are deep within us: 'the whole purpose… is to bring up some lovely solid thing like *living metal* from a world where nothing exists but those inevitable facts.'

I am intrigued by the forest lakes and their connections, if any: some are bog-bound, true locháns of flow country; others have seepages into hollows filled with sphagnum, where running water gets absorbed by the spongy mass. These flows can re-emerge as trickles, though it is doubtful if they could serve as passages for sea trout; others have proper streams chuckling over stones (as is the case with Loch na mBreac), which at the right time of year, with a decent level of water, could bring the 'strangers' [Ted Hughes' poem of this title, in *River* (1983)] up from the sea. So far, two sea trout in May is unusual; I am intrigued by what July and August might bring.

I went to Furnace and delivered sea-trout scales to Elvira; she handed me a bundle of Marine Institute envelopes for more scale samples. The Marine Institute is currently doing DNA studies of those lakes. Analysis of the water can detect the presence of sea trout, but much better information is forthcoming from actual scales. Lough Bunaveela is the only lake with char. (They are smallish, up to about half a pound, judging from her outstretched fingers.)

29th May

The sparrows in the box at the back door fledged today.

Unveiling the Sun

30th May

Five a.m. The spring has been wet and cold. No silage has been cut yet because of the ground conditions so the fields are deep and lush with growth. A few straggling banks of mist disperse from the hollow along the river. The sun is about to rise from under a lid of thin apricot-coloured cloud. The day is still cold. Ahead of the sun, meadow pipits are singing above their territories, the local cock is crowing, and a low grumble of transatlantic flights underscores it all. The may blossom is in its full splendour, a few trees almost totally white.

As I wait for the sun, a fox appears in the garden, mobbed by one of the swallows. It trots along the edge of the rushes, ducking low each time the swallow swoops at it, then disappears into the growth.

By now the neighbour's house on the hill to the east is a low silhouette against a blazing gold sky. While its occupants sleep, a great drama of light is being enacted round it – and I am the only spectator here just now.

At 5:50, the sun appears like a fire at the base of the tree.

June

2nd June

From Letterkeen along the Western Way to Trevor's (near Loch na mBarún) and back. 12.00-17.00.

At first overcast, then brighter, not hot, but we warmed up as we went; midges were a factor when we stopped at the forestry hut to eat a sandwich. A day of sounds above all. Three chiffchaffs between the Raining Trees and the yellow forestry gate where the Western Way branches off to the right.

Willow warblers in the willows to the right of the junction at the end of Correen More. One willow warbler sang in the middle of the plantation near Foxy's, much to Jessica's amusement, contradicting my pronouncement about willow warblers being birds of more open glades.

Blackcaps abundant, you could have counted at least a dozen singers along the track.

Siskins all the time, buzzing.

Crossbills in threes and fives, plus a noisy commotion of these birds high in the spruce trees just along from the forestry hut. Meadow pipit on the open ground under Coire na gCapall. Wren. Robin. Mistle thrush. Hoodie. Raven. Pheasant (Jess saw it cross the track at Foxy's). On the way back, we heard it call – a new species for me so far up. One or two gulls. A heron. A grey wagtail pair near Letterkeen.

No raptors.

Sand martins breeding at Goulaun.

A barn swallow, probably attached to the forestry hut.

Three warbler species: willow warbler, chiffchaff, and blackcap very prominent in the soundscape, and you could probably add grasshopper warbler if you visited at night or at dusk. How very much poorer the experience would be without these African species.

6th June

Went down to Gorteen with Chris and Lynda to find dragonflies and damselflies. Their net was big and ample, the kind of butterfly net you picture with the eccentric naturalists of the 19th century. Within two hours we had a series of new words to attach to the place: blue-tailed damselfly, variable damselfly, large red damselfly and four-spotted chaser. Flowers too: the marsh forget-me-not which grows in damp flushes at the gaps; water avens just coming into flower; and two orchids, common spotted and narrow-leaved marsh orchid. Lynda also caught a small heath butterfly on the damp flats near the lake, a pert, confiding little fellow who sat on my hand and climbed onto my thumbnail before flying off. The blossom on the large hawthorn is over now.

As we came back over the hill we disturbed a large hare from among the oaks. A lapwing pair called right at the top of the hill, still trying to breed there despite magpies and livestock.

8th June

Drove to north Mayo to get news of Paddy McHugh. In Bangor I was given directions to the hospital in Belmullet, where I found him in the old people's home. 'He won't know you,' I was told, and that was indeed the case. He had declined greatly since our last meeting at Tarsaghaun. We walked the corridor together a few times, but he didn't recognise me, and my few attempts at turning conversation to the old themes were fruitless. Then it was time for his tea, so I left, quite upset, wondering whether it was my own vanity or genuine concern for the man that had brought me in the first place.

On the way north, a greenshank flew across the road at Bellaveeny, headed down towards the sea inlet – perfect habitat, and the right time of year, for breeding. I called in at the office in Lagduff to tell them the news.

After my melancholy visit to Belmullet, and an equally melancholy pint in a pub in Bangor, I stopped at Srahnamanragh for an evening's fishing. After a few small parr, and no sign of a decent sea trout, I decided it was best to go. Beautiful aquarelle gradations of ridges and mountains as I drove home through the twilight.

A telephone message when I got back: Lynda asking me to come over to turn their hay with them tomorrow.

10th June

At dusk, an owl flew past the window, flew around briefly at the east end of the house. Probably a barn owl, silent.

The same evening, thirty sparrows in the red willow. They all flew together to avoid a ginger cat.

11th June

The swallows are now feeding their first brood in the porch.

The adults hunt around the house, even making low forays over the lawn at the front in search of insects. This afternoon, a group of house martins spent time prospecting at the eaves – they have turned up before in late spring and even dabbed a few bits of mud at the wall, but always gave up in the end. Presumably the swallows defend our house as their territory. Swifts were hunting below the house today too; all three species were in the air at the same time on this blustery, overcast day.

The whitethroat has now, I believe, found a mate at last.

12th June

We hosted a party for charity, in aid of Brazilian street children. Saturday had been fine but clouds held on stubbornly. Sun came in small allowances all afternoon and evening. One of the guests told me about his father, who is buried in the cemetery overlooking the house. He came from a poorer side of the parish and always looked with longing at our valley, which he called the valley of Joshua, good land owned then by Protestants. Now the man has his plot there at last – six foot under in the graveyard.

14th June

A moderate flood on the river. No sign of a fish. I had a cup afterwards with Pauge and Johnny. We chatted about sundry things:

  the big quartz stone near the road known as a fairy stone; their term for the big quartz blocks here and there on the mountain

  in the old days a man used to come from Glenamoy, selling poitín

  rye was grown for poitín: the guards would look for illegal poitín where rye was grown (straw used for thatch)

some big eels in the locháns. Eels in Loch Dubh, Hughie's lake, which is why cormorants go there.

16th June

A great day on the Owenduff with Lynda and Chris. Lynda got a salmon, about 4lb; I had two: 5lb and 2½lb; Chris had two: 8lb and 6½lb. Chris and I slept in the Blue Lodge the night before. Chris also found a salmon partially eaten by an otter, and took the remainder home.

18th June

Five a.m. Adult and immature lesser black-backed gulls standing in the fields, as if the drumlins were surrounded by sea water. A breeze was up, putting energy into the air, the kind that allows these birds to command space in the valley. A scattered flock of black-headed gulls, all adult birds in breeding plumage, was spread over the silage meadows, hover-hunting for worms, slugs and other invertebrates that had emerged during the night. The ripple of wind in the deep grass and dock leaves made the surface look like water, and the gulls appeared to flit lightly over the meadows, as they do in lakes where they breed. Their forewings were very white, their crowns chocolate brown.

I had come out early, and discovered birds of water quartering the meadows, turning the fields along the river into a rippling, green sea.

The only complaints were from a magpie family chattering in trees and on electricity wires. Any bird sound like this is especially harsh at a time when your nerves are tender from interrupted sleep, and the machine and traffic noises of the human day have not yet filled the world.

An early lark sang above the drumlin of Lugnafahy as I got back to the house.

17th to 18th June

Jessica writes:

For a few days we had become aware of long-eared owls in a copse of trees at the top of the road (between here and the church) where there had been a rookery until a few years ago. We could actually hear the owls' calls from the house at dusk. Our curiosity took us up the road on a few occasions. Seán came back to the house on the 16th very excited as he had seen the owls in flight and in the trees.

I went up on 17th June and took up position near the copse of trees. In a hi-vis jacket and white trousers I hoped drivers would assume I wasn't a burglar and also hoped the house occupants wouldn't part their curtains and see me standing the other side of their garden wall.

Around 10.20 p.m. the owls started calling and replying in excitement(?) and I wasn't surprised to then see (at 10.30 p.m.) two owls fly silently across the top of the meadow to a line of trees opposite their home. Despite the ensuing calls betraying their movements between the copse and the bend at the top of the road, I didn't actually catch sight of them again that evening.

The following evening I was in position by 10.30. The sky was now clear; as a result the owls started calling later and at 10.55 I vowed I'd go home at eleven if I hadn't seen anything. At eleven, as if from nowhere, an owl appeared two arms' lengths away, made eye contact and flew soundlessly to a spot on the wall opposite. I was able to study it through the binoculars for a few minutes, preening, bobbing and calling. A car passed and it flew back up into the trees. I was thrilled of course and texted Seán back at the house.

I didn't go out the following evening (19th) but did on the 20th and was sad to hear nothing at all. They had fledged and gone.

19th June

Re-reading *Notes from Walnut Tree Farm*. So much of Roger Deakin's woodland is about work: hazel coppiced, oak pollarded, hornbeam pleached, hedges laid. English woodland a place of work. Eoghan Daltun's Irish Atlantic rainforest a place of yearning, a source.

21st June

Solstice. Swam in Furnace at 8:00 a.m. with Jess and Eleanor. A salmon jumped; mullet feeding among rocks at the edge. Low water. Pleasant for a swim.

There was very little rain in May, and since early June only a few thundery downpours: a small flood – coloured – in the Owengarve last Monday. I watched the river for a while but saw only tiddlers. Whitethroat and stonechat singing. A cock linnet to cheer me up.

23rd June

The Owenduff flowing moderately at Srahnamanragh. Very bright. Hooked five small finnock below the weir, landed only one. Switched to a double on the point. Found a poacher's net; shredded it with my penknife.

Met Frankie McHugh: he reckoned that if the weather doesn't settle now, approaching the moon's last quarter, the summer will stay unsettled. This year, they had salmon on the Owenmore from early May, the previous year only from July, according to Frankie.

24th June

A foal born last night. Young ravens on fence posts. Most of the meadows now cut. Rooks in companies feeding on the stubble.

25th June

Jessica can text me from China now on her new phone. She writes, 'Lunch. Shall I have old duck of casserole with wring of fruit juice?' Then she's on a twenty-eight-hour train ride from Shanghai to Yichang: 'Bored in my bunk. Still jet-lagged and can't sleep. Chinese are as noisy as Italians but very nice.' My father can't understand this technology and relates such a mystery to the mystery of the expanding universe (into what?).

Three Brazilian friends came for dinner today and to watch Brazil vs Germany on TV. I told my father that what the Irish and Brazilians have most in common is meat. I cooked venison from the Partry House estate for them – a dark, rather tough meat, probably overrated, but you say 'wild meat' to try to add some prestige to the experience. Then forgot to serve the strawberries that I had bought for dessert. So things fall apart when Jessica is away and I prove to be a bad host.

Hay cutters and silage makers are in the meadows now, with people sometimes walking among them, reviving Breugel with their creeping motion on the large canvas of fields and hedgerows.

26th June

Today I am keen to walk a west-east trail through the National Park, from Sheean to the Altnabrocky shelter, taking in a section of the Bangor Trail and then crossing the saddle at Scardaun, between Corslieve and Nephin Beg. While the two existing marked trails, the Bangor Trail and the Western Way, run north-south, there are also sections of trails or paths running at right angles to these, such as the sean bhóthar at Srahduggaun or the track that runs along the Tarsaghaunmore River. I am keen to discover another, or sections of other ways.

Trails on this terrain are not always continuous, like the

Peddars Way in Norfolk as described by Roger Deakin: they 'fizzle out' and then 'pick up their thread' again; they get dispersed in level terrain only to reappear as stony tracks where footfall and hooffall are concentrated, at passing points, or at fords and river crossings, so that on some maps these trails appear as disjointed sections of dotted lines. There is also a finer network of sheep tracks, which can sometimes act as a useful guide to take you along the most comfortable contours of an ascent, or even lead you across a section of swampy ground where these animals have learned the best routes.

Ged and I travel from Newport with Georgia in her shiny new electric vehicle advertising the Dark Sky Park. We then drive past the fishing lodge at Sheean to the end of the track at the Owenduff. Ged presents me with a walking stick for the day, made from a thin gorse stem that has been steam treated into a straight line, with a handle made from antler bone from Rhum, topped with a knob like the eye of a bullock. The day is overcast, mild, and breezy, so there's no threat of midges. Having arranged a pick-up time at the other side with Georgia, Ged and I set out.

A footbridge at this point takes us across to an old cottage and its fields; we then strike out in parallel to a tributary stream flowing out of Gleann Cam (crooked glen), following what is clearly one of the old paths, a rocky track where vegetation has been worn away by people, cattle, ponies, donkeys and sheep. The surface of glacial drift is littered with an assortment of boulders, including some bright lumps of quartz that have been rounded by abrasion in the glacial outwash and light our way, like beacons. Then everything thins out, the trail disappears, and, as if to compensate, our conversation quickens – we haven't met for a while.

Gleann Cam, between Slieve Alp and Marafach, has a lovely tributary stream, like a blade of silver, running through it. Our feet move across a sibilance of molinia, black bog rush and deer grass. Molinia forms knee-high tussocks across the valley floor, which would make for heavy going, so we stay on the higher shoulder under Slieve Alp. We head for Sceilg na gCon (crag of the hound), a low hill at the head of the valley, crowned by a rocky outcrop, like a tor. Then the trail reappears, taking us down to a stream crossing at the foot of this hill, and then fades out again as we climb the southern shoulder out of Gleann Cam to get our first view of the Owenduff catchment. The first, awestruck impression here is of space, distance and emptiness; but then the eye – and our conversation – fixes on detail: the thin seam of the Bangor Trail running along the foot of the mountain; the white cascade of Scardaun; the craggy sides of a corrie under Glennamong summit. Then, out on the valley floor, two kilometres away, my binoculars find scaffolding and building materials at Teach Pháidín, a ruined cottage I visited many years ago. This renovation project is the latest in a series designed to provide shelter for walkers in the most remote locations of the National Park.

   Somewhat closer than that, among a patchwork of old fields (in Irish, tamhnaigh) just below the Bangor Trail, is a livestock enclosure that I am keen to see again. This place, Tamhnach na Sifín (anglicised as Tamlesheffaun), gives its name to the southern shoulder of Corslieve. Sifín in the placename at first suggests stems of straw, perhaps, if oats or rye were grown here, but I'm also distracted today by stems of deer grass and other sedges that proliferate. In any case, the sifín of this place, by a familiar process of alignment, has been promoted to the mountain overhead, in the name Tamlesheffaun.

   The enclosure is a loose figure of eight, comprising two pens, with gates for sorting animals. A section of the stone has been restored with a mortar mixture of lime and river sand. Atop another wall, a layer of sods – 'scraws' in local parlance – has bedded in and bonded seamlessly, and now softens the appearance of the stone-work, like a piece of green architectural design.

    This enclosure was originally sited across the bed of a stream, and a culvert was built at the base of the wall to allow water to flow across the floor, so that cattle held here overnight en route to market were able to drink. This double enclosure is empty now, but there's still an echo, a reverberation from days when this place was alive with the commotion of drovers and their animals, and the nearby cultivation ridges were thick with the foliage of potatoes, cabbage and fodder crops that helped stock survive the winter. A litter of discarded sweet wrappers and plastic bottles tells of more recent business involving sheep; these yards are still in use, and carefully maintained.

    We continue on, following the trail south towards Scardaun. The trail swings left, under Tamlesheffaun; we cross the rocky course of a stream flowing from the bowl of Log an Fhia (hollow of the deer), the name marking a species that became extinct in this area in the 19th century, to be reintroduced at the end of the 20th. The water here runs vigorously through its black bed and dances over the lips of rocks as glittering gouts of exuberance. We think that this water, emerging from the bedrock, should be safe to drink, unlike the slow-moving, peaty fiodáns of the valley bottom. We find two builder's bags, full of sand, from a chopper drop several years ago for some purpose that is now obscure. The plastic fabric is disintegrating; white scraps that the wind and weather have worn out of the fabric litter the stones here.

    We stop for lunch at Burke's, in an old shed built here some years ago within the walls of a ruined cottage. I know from a conversation with the McHughs at Tarsaghaun that the last man to live here would walk to Tarsaghaun and borrow a pony for the trip to Bangor to buy flour. He would then return to Tarsaghaun and carry the bag of flour the rest of the way home.

The fine stone structures at this farm or 'living' show that it was not just a seasonal booley, but a year-round settlement, with a lean-to for hens, a haggard for storage, and a neatly enclosed hay meadow.

Ged pours hot water from a Stanley thermos flask and we drink peppermint tea with our sandwiches, sitting in this decaying workman's hut where the floor sheeting has rotted out to reveal a set of foundations built using creosoted railway sleepers. The thermos flask, Ged reckons, was one of the greatest advances in technology; I counter with the story of an old perforated, square biscuit tin and a blackened kettle that my parents took on our outings to the Burren. Burning a small bundle of twigs in the tin was enough to boil water for our tea. Maybe it was my mother who felt that this roadside arrangement made us look needy and who was responsible for the eventual upgrade to thermos flasks.

We linger for a while to pay a kind of homage to the abandoned fields and enclosures, and find another badger sett dug into the sandy soil within a palisade of rushes. After a final time-check and a call to Georgia, we step off the trail and climb the saddle at Scardaun where a banner of white water drapes the hillside; this outflow from the Scardaun lakes is visible from several miles away after heavy rain, acting like a beacon to signal to the angler that the rivers are running high, and that the fishing is 'on'.

The wind, funnelled across this high saddle between Tamlesheffaun and Nephin Beg, stirs the lakes' surface to an angry commotion and cancels any thought of paddling, let alone swimming. We stride along, conversing about grasses and sedges, admiring the abundance and the attractive flowers of deer grass, the sifín of this place. The beautiful, tousled cream stamens of the flower are arrayed like a contemporary chandelier in the lobby of a posh hotel. Ged spots a golden plover for an instant, flitting away ahead of us.

As we pass the lakes and drop down off the saddle, the Nephin Forest is in the valley beneath us, its vibrant green tide marking a new phase of this landscape's history. A discreet gap in the trees takes us down to the forestry track leading to the Altnabrocky shelter. As well as the usual small store of provisions, someone has left a substantial measure of whiskey and a bright new sleeping mat. I see a puddle of vomit on the ground under the picnic table; perhaps the same whiskey disgreed with this walker. There's no sign of the favourite hazel walking stick I left here in February.

Mizzle and mist have set in from the west as we walk out to meet Georgia at five o'clock. At one minute past, her white KIA appears, which we think is pretty good timing for Altnabrocky, or anywhere.

27th June

One of the draft fishermen at Gweesalia, near Bangor, says that there are big spring salmon in the estuary, a sign that there will be a flood in a few days' time. He was speaking on Friday, and predicted a flood on Monday. Rain did come on the Monday. Fish ran on Tuesday and Wednesday in the Clew Bay rivers.

30th June

The Owenduff is very low, full of weed. I parked near Sheean Lodge and walked a mile downstream. Picked some cherries from a tree near a ruined house. Chris rang me, and advised going to the weir at Srahnamanragh. I arrived at sundown, with light to tackle up comfortably in. The tide had just peaked. I had a few little finnock from the stream at the weir – no fish more than 5oz. As dusk gathered, I moved a hundred yards farther down and here I caught a good many little sea trout, of similar size. Things were very busy for forty minutes or so, while there was enough water to keep the fish up in the river, but then things went very quiet, and by twelve o'clock the tide had drained out, the meagre river had returned to its freshwater state, and there seemed little prospect of further fish. During the busy period a few big fish had appeared, grilse or sea trout.

As it gets dark, it becomes hard to judge distances. Swish swish goes the fly line. You launch into darkness and hope that you are near the rise that you heard, but saw only vaguely. The mouth of the river is packed with sea trout, but June was very dry this year and they have had no opportunity to run. There are a few salmon in the river, about one fish in each of the major pools, but grilse are largely absent so far because of the lack of water.

I am told that over forty spring salmon were caught on the Owenduff this year – a very good tally.

3rd July

To the Ballycroy café, Ginger and Wild, in the afternoon with a consignment of books. The Owengarve largely fallen away, but the Owenduff is still in good order as I drive on from Ballycroy. A clearance, then another shower blurring out Corslieve as I park. A chaffinch pecking in Paude's yard.

No cars parked anywhere. I think I have the place to myself. Every time I come here it is as if I have managed to shake off all obligations, to home, to loved ones, even to work. One reason why I write now, if not to capture the feeling of truancy at this end point, at least to salvage some modicum of duty or profit. By writing, I am trying to behave as if this were work, though I know there's nothing better than this.

Speckling of rain still on the car, but it's time to go – upstream – where I should have a fly on the water in half an hour. I am going back to the scene of great days, especially that outing with Michael Kingdon, our first on the river.

I fish above the footbridge reverentially – nothing. Then at Huxley's pool, tempted by the prospect of a salmon (this is not what I am here for) – nothing. Blank at two more spots, then, at the sea trout flat, I change to a lighter line (mustn't spook) because the splash of a double hook is too much. A stoat's tail on the point. I back up with a strong breeze behind me – nothing; then I turn to fish down and get one, a three-quarter-pound silvery fish landed after a minute or two steering round the pool, take a scale for the Marine Institute, then nurse the fish back slowly after its shock. It gradually recovers, its frog gape panting, then kicks away.

A squall comes on from Achill. I put the notebook away.

Two fish from the Black Flats at the junction (a stream off the bog joins the river here). Both fresh. Both about three-quarters of a pound. Dragged in and dumped back quickly – they rattled away.

Alterations of cloud and light in a jostling breeze. Sand martins along the river. Corslieve blue-silver ('gorm'). A very lonely emptiness above me. By the time I reach the Black Flats, I get a feeling that I have arrived, even though there's another hour's walking to reach the base of Corslieve and the Abhainn Gharbh. At the Black Flats I am at a summit, not of altitude, but of distance: there's a similar light-headedness here, looking towards the massif of Corslieve, or the diagonal belt of the Tamlesheffaun ridge in front of it.

Bright again. I sit at the island pool above the weather gauge, waiting for the black-and-white world that must come; a toiling mortar of grey cloud above the forestry to the north will be my ally. Sea trout are nocturnal in essence: their night passage. Colour draining from the world to reveal their silver – a no-colour, a purity, a light of the sea hiding in the bog.

As the dusk falls, the streams take on an oily, viscous appearance. My fly probes them, and on a couple of occasions there's the boil and pluck of a sea trout (of about a pound), but this time none of them is hooked, the fly comes away. At this stage, I wonder if my own fatigue is influencing my ability to catch these creatures. There's a nausea here also, the obverse of the feeling of elation that comes with having the upper reaches of the river to myself and of catching three sea trout in this remote setting. Fatigue, surfeit, and a doubt about staying on so late, to see if dusk will deliver more action, combine in my mind to detract from my concentration. How come I lose three or four, with a double hook on the point, when I got three out of three earlier in the evening?

With rain coming in again (from the Achill direction, with the pyramid of Slievemore on the horizon, and Paul Henry towers of grey overhead) the evening is slipping away from me. I have no energy left to concentrate on any more sport; the darkening bogs and midges are monstrous, like a threat of storm in *King Lear*. My thoughts are turning to home, and comforts. Camping out here now would be wretched: I'd need to be well equipped to bivouac at the bothy, even with its secure roof.

A heavy squall hits me as I pass Sweeney's; water is streaming from my leggings and jacket as I reach the car. I struggle into the passenger seat, where I change before switching to the driver's seat. Weary on the drive back. How we live by our comforts, routines and stories; how inhospitable the bare hillsides are without the pegs of language and warmth to get us across them. This is true even now, in midsummer, when the dawn light will be breaking across the Nephins in five hours' time.

For all this, I have learned something more of the river, seen it in another mood. Questions: how old are these three-quarter pounders? Are they finnock? Can they have grown to this size in a few months since going to sea at the smolt stage a few months ago? Have they not wintered at sea, like grilse?

Coming down to the main road towards Ballycroy, flashing lights and a big vehicle – a forestry truck and a garage recovery vehicle, as incongruous there, then, as a fairground in the desert. The banal fact of a forestry truck needing assistance because of a breakdown, still an extraordinary appearance.

5th July

I think about the expanse of the upper river as a brooding mass still holding on to its secrets. The angler goes there with hopes, with the urge to wrestle something from that place in the form of a few fish, and manages that, but all the time the place takes its toll on him, the weather and midges pester him, the scale of the land saps his energies, the hunt for fish comes at a cost: his composure, his ambitions to be master of the place, but as night falls and the rainclouds reclaim Corslieve, another series of presences overwhelms him, like a set of unanswered questions about light and darkness, the appearance of water in the small hours, the behaviour of birds early in the morning, that unidentified cry from a higher valley – a fox, was it? Some hunted creature going about its business with no inkling that anyone were there to hear its shout at the scree, and then the cattle that are here in summer resolving reds and whites into appearance after the brief intermission of a midsummer night showing that this valley, for all its remoteness, is territory for a farmer's livestock, as it has been in summer since at least the 18th century; these cattle, like the sheep you see dragging heavy fleece across the fords, tell you about economy, and subsidy schemes, and the mendacity that goes with stocking levels in these parts.

6th July

On the Owenduff above the junction, the river in lovely order after a spate. I hit my first grilse in a fast glide about a mile above the junction: he took the dropper fly, a sparsely tied dunkeld. No net, so I had to play and then drag him into shingle at the top of the pool. 3¾lb, in a beautiful setting. Later, at the top of the beat, I found a long flat, deep and dark, where the fly-fishing seemed hopeless, but a fish was stirring towards the tail of the pool. On the fifth or sixth cast he took, and within about five minutes I had him on a little sandy bank within twenty metres of where he had struck. Five pounds. The trek back to the car with nearly ten pounds of salmon was exhausting, but I was exhilarated to have 'cracked it' after so many blank days.

13th July

Our brood of swallows flew for the first time this morning. Parents still feeding them; now they are back on the nest. Six young this year. The first brood failed: a male adult died and the female took a new partner who pushed his predecessor's almost incubated eggs from the nest, so she had to start again.

15th July

Went up Tarsaghaun More with Fergal. The river was low after a flood the previous week. We met a Marine Institute scientist who was not impressed when I asked jovially if she had seen any salmon, as we had a net and 'were anxious to get a few'.

We walked up to Glendeegan, to the last two houses, and followed the river on to where it runs through a series of little gullies with basins and short falls of water between them. The side of one gully had only very recently collapsed, leaving a heap of rocks in the pool below, and a large holly tree lying on its side in the water. Large dragonflies, like helicopters in an Alpine valley, patrolled up and down these narrow defiles.

After that we left the river and climbed to the top of Corslieve. The grass, sedges and heather seem to be gradually recovering after the worst years of overgrazing, although the heather is scarcely tall enough yet to offer cover for grouse, and the bilberry plants are tiny. From the summit, the upper half of the Tarsaghaunmore is like a textbook river, meandering in wide loops like a varicose vein across the glen. A wheatear flitted about as we ate our sandwiches.

On our way back, we stopped at Casadh na Leice to watch for salmon – and sure enough, one broke in the tail of the pool, the spreading rings of the rise like the eye of the land itself. We saw him break several times with, once or twice, a great angry movement of the tail.

17th July

Annagh, with Jessica and Yvonne. A warm, bright day. We reached the saddle within forty minutes and were down at the lake in little over an hour. Loch na gCaorόg was very still, a deep gentian blue; the sea was lighter blue, with corrugations of wave undulations sweeping across from the north-west. The news this morning was of seabed searches for wreckage from R116, but the sea looks agitated: strong detonations of white spray from the base of Slievemore and the western end of Duvillaun.

We went down the stony track slowly, chatting as we went, examining ankle-break holes carefully and circumventing them. Lots of meadow pipits twitching on the heather, and many marbled moths dancing across the heather tips. The lake surface punctuated with small beetles motoring about. One small, minnow-sized fish.

When we came to the brow of the moraine overlooking the boulder beach, we discovered several sheep on the rocks by the shore: they had not been shorn and must have sweltered under those shaggy fleeces. The path eastward towards Annagh Strand is level, but here and there are a few gaps in the rocks that could trap an unwary walker. One set of recent boot marks on the path. At the bothán, we saw a man on the ridge above us who had passed by as we were parking the car. Nettles around the bothán had been cut to allow access to the enclosure. The heavy smell of nettles an aftermath of the days when people lived here and grew potatoes during the summer. Someone had gathered a few logs and a pallet at a fireplace, the idyll no doubt interrupted by midges.

A common sandpiper called at the beach: its footprints at the top of the sand were the only marks preceding us. There is a scree slope a little way to the east which could hold breeding Manx shearwaters – worth searching for. Jessica looked at the breaking waves with their soup of weed and churned sand for a while, but in the end we elected to paddle, with the froth running around our feet. A dizzy feeling as the glassy ground slid away from us. Now and again a heavier wave caught us up to the knees. We were like clients of a nature-based therapy service; reflexology on a deserted beach.

The quartzite stones and boulders have been worn and rounded by the action of the sea: you can hear boulders being rolled around along the stony sections. They are whitish, rounded like eggs, rugby balls, pillows, sometimes with a dark dense pinstripe. Dried kelp rods are twisted among these stones like fleeing snakes. The trunk of a conifer, with its root base scuffed and worn: a club for a giant such as Dáithí Bán. My trophy was a blue rope, enough for Pozzo to keep Lucky tethered by, and a piece of insulation material that might have come from a lost helicopter. Several drinks bottles, and other plastics: something that looked like a loo – with a view. A large buoy from a lobster pot.

At the face of the moraine, freshwater seeping down has dark moss growing, and an unusual plantain, very pale and delicate in the dark grotto. We kept going to the eastern end of the lake and found many marbled moths dead on the water surface at the margin. Old otter spraint. We could have found more, fresher, if we had looked.

A brisker pace on the return. Vegetation in good order on this sheltered side of the island. Tall heather on the slopes over Loch na gCaoróg, but still no sign of a grouse. We pick our way back up the track to the top of the saddle, less talk, more intent on the journey. One break: a red lobster boat comes from the west, moving among the buoys. It rounds on one and winches the yellow bead on board, revving as it does, emitting bursts of white water. A ribbon of foam extends all along the shore under Slievemore and as far as Annagh beach, like a Zen master's flourish with a white brush. The tide has withdrawn and the impact at the foot of the shore is less pronounced.

We get back to the car at about five o'clock; less than six hours in all. After coffee in Keel, Jess, Yvonne and I join the holidaymakers in the waves. Great bursts of joy in the breakers.

18th July

My river is a favourite place, a rocky avenue of shallows twisting across a lonely bog with a few bigger holding pools where fish might stay in the months prior to spawning. There are no lakes draining its course, only a motley scattering of bog pools slowly leaking water into the peat. Rain brings sudden flushes of water into the river, and once that stops the levels fall away just as rapidly.

The most violent spates have knocked big chunks of peat out of the riverbank and washed rubble, gravel and clay out of the lower levels where they had settled after the action of glaciers during the Ice Age. These deposits have been sifted by water and brought to quieter currents, where sediments form gravel banks and sandy pastures all along the stream. Plants such as gorse, which hate the soggy conditions of the open bog, can grow here, as can grass; and where grass grew, people were tempted into the valleys in search of grazing for their livestock.

When there is water, July is the best time for sea trout. Rain had come as forecast, starting in the evening and continuing overnight. Just as crucially, the rain was due to stop in the morning, so that the flood would peak, and then run off during the day. A big, falling flood is the optimal time. This allows a window of a few hours when fish are agitated, eager to snatch at novelties swimming through the water. If you miss that window, as I have done many times, there's a melancholy feeling that the few fish you stir are stragglers from a glamorous party now ending – one to which you were not invited.

On my way north through clearing showers I had an eye on the streams running under the road: quiet, modest little rivers usually veiled by alders and hazels were now a big agitation of brown water and froth. The powerful mass of seawater would swallow these freshwater streams in due course; grey-brown distances of gently profiled ridges had absorbed the night's rain into anonymity. Here and there across the hills, cataracts formed white lines of fresh floodwater plunging down steep slopes. My need was acute, to be assured by such signs that the water was still running high, that the spate would not have drained away before I got there. The sight of the main river dispelled all doubt: it was a monster struggling to get under the bridge and away to the sea. There would be more than enough water; I was not going to miss the flood; there might even be a crushing surfeit of brown water, making angling impossible for a while.

When the two biggest rivers in this region are in spate, there is no chance of fishing, and the anglers put away all thought of sport until the following day. But on my river there is a narrow window after the flood has peaked, which I have rarely managed to get to; I thought, the time is now, and I must keep going.

Timing the flood was one thing; the other was a decision to make once I had parked the car: should I go upstream or down?

Downstream, the river runs past a conifer plantation into a narrow cutting; there are two large pools here, with a long history of poaching, and several faster runs where I have often encountered sea trout, but this lower section of the river lacks the elemental loneliness of the upper stretches. I decided to go upstream.

A low bluff 300 metres away from the parking place gave me the first proper view of the river as it ran in a shallow stream between a high peat bank on one side, and a level green space the size of a football pitch. There was a soundscape here too, of streaming, chuckling, growling, the running total of a night's rain off the deserted mountain. Every leaking peat bank, every gargling fiddaun, every stony drain, every gravelled stream, pouring, trickling, dribbling, dripping, seeping, surging, cascading, drifting, becoming this restive, unfamiliar creature of the wilderness.

In these conditions the river is alive in a special sense: you know that salmon and sea trout are running. There is not much to eat in these barren waters – salmon don't feed here at all; it's the breeding instinct that brings these fish into the narrow, hazardous channel of the river, where they risk their fortunes for a few months before spawning time. Somewhere in this rush of cold water there are streamlined, cold-blooded muscles of protein making their way against the flow, their backs perfectly camouflaged from predators. Occasionally, you hear a splash as a salmon crosses a shallow place, but by the time you turn to look, it has vanished into the turbulence.

I walked down the stony track and continued on briskly towards a ruined, roofless cottage half a mile away. A small tributary stream was so full that I had to make a wide detour in order to get across it. At the cottage itself I sat within the walls and set up my three-piece rod and flies, even though I had not yet come to the pool where I hoped to start. The river was still virtually unfishable; water was toiling and twisting through the big pools, preventing fish from holding their positions; they would be lodged at the bottom somewhere, in the shelter of a rock, until falling levels gave them back their world. Sea trout like areas of smooth current; they avoid the churning effect of high floods.

Close to the cottage, where the stream ran through old pasture, the flood had brimmed out over submerged silvery grass blades. Here I marked the level with a stick as a reference for later.

Then I took up my rod and kept going, crossing wet, peaty trenches, stepping on heathery tufts in the softer, sphagnum-filled sections. The river was the only mark in a vast, wide bowl of blanket bog rising to a smooth horizon of mountain ridges several kilometres away. The slow drift of cloud shadow on these slopes knew nothing of my agitation; it also seemed to have forgotten the rain that had fallen, a story that was now gathered in the stream.

In its upper reaches the river meanders in wide, varicose loops, textbook style, across the valley floor. There are memorials here, cabins and enclosures from booleying days, but I am a poor guide to them because the angler is fixated on the hunt for fish and has little curiosity for other things. The stony flanks of the mountain loom high above these deserted expanses as you approach the top of the catchment. Water drains rapidly off these slopes; floodwaters do not stay high for long once the rain stops. I look at the upper reaches and wonder how far sea trout go? They are famous for running high into catchments. I have dreamt of sea trout trying to get up mountainsides on the shooting spurt of a cascade. But even these great migrants have their limits, and once the smaller streams lose their floodwater, the sea trout will fall back to the deeper stretches.

I eventually reached the biggest pool in the upper stretch and studied the prospects. A broken stream runs into it at a shallow angle and turns sharply at the foot of a crag forming its western side. The deep water holds salmon and sea trout, a famous spot for poaching and angling where I have caught sea trout and grilse. Most of the pool was a boiling mass of slightly coloured water, all topsy-turvy from the volume of the flow, but at the tail, just before the current fell away into another fast run, there was a glassy stretch of several metres where the water flowed evenly. I cast the flies across the pool and let them swing into the smooth glaze of the pool tail. A fish rose but did not take. I tried again, and again a sea trout boiled at the fly without making contact. A few casts later, as I worked the same spot, a bigger fish locked onto the fly and held it down in the depths. It must have been a grilse or a very big sea trout, because it did not show, but moved slowly upstream into the churning commotion. A fine 'v' spread out from the taut fly line where it entered the water. Then the line anchored on the bottom and would not budge. I suppose that the second fly, which hangs on a dropper off the main line, had snagged on a tuft of vegetation. There was nothing doing when I tried to coax it off again, so I had to pull with my hands until the line gave way and I pulled in the remains of the leader, minus fish and flies. I would have to tie on another set of lures and start again.

As I did, I saw signs that the water was dropping: fragments of moss and rushes washed up by the flood had got caught on the growth and were already a few inches proud of the river. Falling water levels, fish in the river, a respite from midges, and total solitude: the day was shaping up as one of those rare occasions, which happen just a few times a year, perhaps, when all variables are favourable to a drama of silver fish in dark water.

When it flows out of the big pool, the river enters a series of fast streams and then follows a straight, narrow channel for a few hundred metres, with a high peat bank on the right, and a flat stretch of pasture on the left. Here the channel deepens and the river flows for the last hundred metres before it enters another deep pool and swings left. This straight stretch should be a sea trout angler's dream, and I have fished it many times with great hopes and little reward. These dark waters tantalise and challenge; just as you decide that the prospects are hopeless, a vigorous 'schtock' exploding near your fly, but not taking, reminds you that there is life in the cold, peaty element, and the moment evades you even as it is offered.

With the river running so high, I had to approach this stretch from the top of the peat bank; I was forced to clamber over peat hags and down onto a few grassy ledges where you can work the line from a low position. (If you stand high on the bank, your figure looms on the horizon and you easily spook these shy fish.) The stream was a truculent body of water hurtling through its course, the swing of the line was too brief, and the current too rapid; I had to move farther down, to a final fifty metres where the current slackens in a deeper, somewhat wider stretch. A deep drain cuts through the peat bank at this point and joins the river: this confluence of streams is a special, favoured place for sea trout; the black mystery of this water renders the sudden appearance of a glittering sea trout a miraculous revelation.

My flies had a little more time here to take their course across the current, where their tufts of sooty black fluff with glints of silver might tempt the hungry creatures. After a couple of casts, two sea trout exploded at the leader, taking to the air as their mouths discovered the hooks. Both flies had been hit simultaneously. The fish went down, the reaction was sluggish at first, but then the movement was fluid, a single gesture, and it was clear that one of the fish had come off. The remaining one, weighing about a pound, came to my hand easily a couple of minutes later.

Sea trout in this river run in floods from June onwards and are due to spawn in November, but they can be curiously shy or absent when there is no recent rainwater to agitate them. Many watchers of these rivers believe that they return to the estuaries and bays where they can feed. Unlike brown trout, sea trout are not active surface feeders in fresh water; there is little to keep them nourished in these bog streams. The sudden appearance of an angler's fly must be as mysterious to them as a mirage to a delirious desert traveller. When the angler's fly swims into a pool, or lands on the surface, these fish do not have to be coaxed into taking, though their mood can be overly aggressive or desultory.

I now had a fish in my bag, and trout slime on my hands; that, along with the anecdote of a bigger fish lost, was enough to ensure that the day was 'on'. The angler, though, is rarely content, and usually hurries to the next pool after taking his first fish. The long, straight run drains into a deep, stomach-shaped pool which then curves to the left in a narrow flow; the main current stays close to a high bank on the right, but at its centre the pool is calmer, and this is the best place to present the fly. I did so, and a trout took instantly; it joined the other in my bag.

The river's course changes after this section and is no longer shadowed by a high peat bank on one side. Instead, it has flat pasture on both sides and the rim of the riverbank is scarcely two feet above the water. While this section is easy to access, the lack of cover means that the angler looms on the horizon as a monster of the moor, so his approach must be cautious. There's one beautiful stretch here, a long, broad pool that settles quickly after the agitation at its entrance. For me it is the quintessential moorland pool for sea trout.

Here I felt compelled to look up and around, and take in the day. The mountain top was draped with a steam-train puff of cloud; lower cloud formed a grey distance, but the sun was now dominating a blue sky. On the normal scale of variables, brightness is a setback for the sea trout angler. If water conditions are not optimal – as they were now – direct sunlight is a curse and puts off all but a few fish. You can toil all day in a well-stocked river with hardly a stir and, as your frustrations increase, you come to hate the river and everything associated with the hunt. One bright day I dragged my line for hours through tea-coloured water in the shadow of the wind farm at Bellacorick and despaired of the naivety that had brought me there, and the tenacity of my companion, which kept me there. But there are some sunny days when the river is alive with taking fish, when every pool and run has a grilse, a sea trout, or even a brownie knocking at the fly, when the sun loses its power and all the angler has to do is present the fly discreetly.

I stood back from this favourite pool and took a few photographs of the landscape as I waited for some cloud cover. Then a threadbare screen of mist veiled the sun for an interval, giving me a chance to cast. One fish took, and came away from the hook after a few lurches; then another took the fly, and was hooked securely. When I got this one in my hand, a certain scruple took over and I gave it back to the water as an offering, to the planet, to the river, to some ad hoc household god.

Something in me relaxed at this point; I was no longer anxious about catches and tallies as I followed the river down for another kilometre, crunching across gravelly levels, or thudding softly on the grassy margin of the stream. The water was clear, the day brighter than I would have liked, but sea trout continued to take, in all the usual runs, including one big fish that steered my line around the depth of a pool for a couple of minutes before the hook flew up and he was gone.

Several more trout came to the fly and made brief contact before I lost them; there was a margin of hesitation in their behaviour that day which I could not explain. On other days the fish took the fly with more savage urgency and these were more likely to hook themselves securely.

I made my last careful stop at a big pool in this upstream section. The heavy flank of a salmon turned strongly close to the fly without making contact. I could have changed my lure, put on one of the bigger, proven salmon patterns in my box, but I chose not to, and fished on, still in pursuit of sea trout; here I caught my fourth fish of the day, another pounder which rattled onto the stony margin of the river.

The mark I had made earlier with a stick was now a foot and a half above the water level; the flood was running down rapidly, but there were still a couple of hours' fishing until dusk for anyone with the energy to continue.

And there was also the option of night fishing for sea trout.

Some anglers such as Hugh Falkus, and a few in my locality, prefer to fish for sea trout at night, when their behaviour changes, and they move more freely about the pools under cover of darkness. In his book, *Sea Trout Fishing* (1962), Falkus describes setting out in pursuit of these fish only when the sun is declining, with no thought of casting a line before the sun is off the water. This nocturnal sport amounts to total acquiescence to the sun curse, and involves many hours alone, indifferent to family ties. I know of one group whose annual fishing holiday to north Mayo is completely focussed on night fishing.

There are sea trout rivers in Wales where fishing at night is not unusual, and where anglers on busy beats will pass each other as blurry shadows with muted voices. In north Mayo, on the other hand, a night angler has to confront the demon of utter solitude, with very few echoes from others who have trod the same path. The angling writer Sidney Spencer is one of the few who have broached this darkness in a western Irish setting, in an essay on 'Seatrout at Night' from his book *Newly from the Sea* (1969). 'The darkened river is another world,' he wrote, 'Its sights are hidden, its scents and voices intensified… The sound of a river in the night is one of the greatest sounds in nature.' What these intensified voices might amount to, Spencer does not say; a different, more literary writer might be tempted to examine this suggestion and follow its hauntings, but angling writers such as he and Falkus are totally focussed on the pursuit of fish. These hauntings, I suggest, are the point at which most of us balk, and retreat, as Ted Hughes did in his poem on the nocturnal hunt for sea trout, 'August Evening'. He describes the cold, alienating experience of being out on the river on an early autumn night: 'Wet fog midnight, / A sheathing sea-freeze, hardens round my head, / Stiffens my fingers.' Even though the river is well stocked – 'the sea tribes are here' – he is overwhelmed by the exposure, declares that 'The river is terrible' and decides to go home.

At such moments most of us need reassurance when confronted with the unfamiliar bog at night. For now, though, night fishing for sea trout on Mayo's spate rivers is a story that has very few witnesses; the intensified voices of Spencer's river at night is a frontier for others to explore.

25th July

Jess and I left after lunch to go to Tubbrid. The forecast said overcast, no rain – though the clouds were inclined to break up. Took the Nephin Drive via Srahmore. The streams much reduced since the weekend's rain.

Peacock butterflies freshly emerged all along the track, starting near the wooden entrance gate to the National Park. A few ringlets, a green-veined white. Lots of large dragonflies along the track, as before, small damselflies and darters, including a glassy, translucent species that is easily missed. You sometimes hear a papery rustle from the wings of the larger ones. Four big dragonflies in the air at one time.

Then two young bucks on the track: they moved to the right

Unveiling the Sun

margin: in the slant of sunlight you saw the velvety growth on their new antlers. One animal, single-pointed; the other three-pointed. They had moved off into the forest as we came past.

Everything very quiet now: an occasional bird call (goldcrest, chaffinch, wren, robin, siskin, crossbill). No corvids except the raven (and occasionally a jay) venture in here.

The track marked by deer prints and a couple of tyre tracks, plus my own boot marks from two days ago.

We stepped off the track to view Loch Geal. Jessica took the binoculars from me to scan the area, and said, 'It's a sea eagle, I can see a sea eagle, have a look, Seán, to check.' I said, 'No, you're having me on. I don't believe you.' Jessica said, 'It's not April fool. There, above the small tree, he's right there.' She handed me the binoculars, 'You can even see it with the naked eye.'

And there it was, perched half-way up a lodgepole by the lake shore, a sea eagle, the massive yellow bill showing in profile, like the bald eagles that have been photographed thus many times in places like Alaska. It continued to sit there, though it must have seen us; it was thrilling that we had seen it before it flew off. This one had heavy pale streaking around the upper body. A white plume drifted about in the air in front of it – one of its own preenings? Our squabbling, even, had not disturbed it.

Then, after a minute or more, the eagle took off as I had the glasses on it, a flash of a wing tag, a white tail, a mature bird. It seemed massive, heavy and vigorous as it disappeared into the trees, and did not show again, although a flicker of shadow on the ground near me could have been caused by these eagle wings crossing the sun.

This eagle, apparently at home in what I have always thought of as excellent habitat, felt like a fulfilment, a confirmation of all the days out in north Mayo in recent years, with my gaze regularly turned to the sky, like the devoted yearning of a pilgrim. 'It can only get better,' I said, 'next thing will be to see a pair of them.' Perhaps sea eagles were breeding here already, or had established a territory, without our knowing.

We walked on, and two more deer appeared briefly, crossing the track in the distance, having seen us. The day was crowding with impressions, dragonflies abundant in the air above us. I showed Jessica Loch na mBreac. By now we were tired, elated, and did not feel the need to explore any farther.

Then, near the wooden entrance gate, a curious mewing, snarling sound coming from a belt of conifers, like nothing I had heard before, making me think of 'cat crainn', the Irish for pine marten. This extra revelation was in keeping with such a day buzzing with life.

A cat on a boreen near the gate – could it have provoked the pine marten to the screams and agitation?

31st July

On the river. High water, dropping. Something burnished, unsteady about the water. Two fish hooked and lost. Otherwise blank. Paude also touched and lost three. Hard work. Fish not inclined.

A few bursts of sunlight just as I fished some favourite spots.

Felt low. We fish and fish until we have exhausted the thing we love, and ourselves with it.

No sign of Corslieve in the gloom. Just a scrap of light on a hillside occasionally, when the sun found a gap in the cloud.

A gable-end stands.
A fence collapsed at the bridge.
Dragonflies dancing.

August

6th August

Peter McGroary sent me a video a couple of weeks ago of a sea eagle over Bellacragher Bay with ravens in attendance.

    I set out to follow the old trail from Claggan to Loch an Aifrinn (Jessica had discovered this trail emerging at the end of the lake) and parked up near the creek. Once I left the road and stepped over the barbed wire fence, the noise of traffic diminished. The glacier has left rolling waves of drift running parallel to the ridge of the mountain. I stepped up to the top of the first of these and continued into the landscape's embrace, distances opening up, always greater than at first imagined. In the first hollow behind this ridge, having crossed the fiodán, I floundered through wet bog with bog myrtle for a hundred metres. Climbing again at the far side, I see that I've missed a small booley site a small way to my left.

    The trail, comprised of discontinuous sections that are easy to lose, takes me up in zig-zag. There's a high transverse going around the spur which looms between me and Loch an Aifrinn. Streams have cut steep little gullies into the flanks of the moraines, forming narrow sanctuaries for vegetation out of the wind's reach, away from the cropping teeth of sheep.

The loose geometry of the trail leads me higher. I stop to photograph a distinct stretch of bare track, then look up – and there it is, at first just a dark ripple, a tiny signature against the clouds, then, as it approaches overhead, it comes into itself, into the lens of my binoculars, looms like a crucifixion, like some ritual angel dressed in finery; the primaries are splayed, separated to grip the air, the line of secondaries is tattered, gappy (this must be the moult) and the tail's lozenge is distinct.

Without beating its wings, as there's a steady breeze to keep it lifted along the flank of the ridge, it wheels around a few times in a wide loop centred on me. This is the first time I am aware of being scrutinised by a sea eagle; a juvenile at Letterkeen saw me and fled, but this bird is examining a new thing that has moved into its territory, which is now lying there, prone in its rain jacket, swearing in exuberant elation.

Then a squadron of ravens appears around it, and begins the usual routine of harassment. I was dismayed at the swarm of corvids pursuing my first Mayo sea eagle at Ballinrobe; this pestering was more nonchalant: most of the birds dropped away after a couple of minutes, the last two quickly lost interest as well, leaving this eagle alone in the sky once again. This bird, I thought, has been here for a while: the ravens are used to it, it is no longer a novelty.

I watched the eagle turn east and drift away towards Loch an Aifrinn, rounding the spur I was heading towards, and thought, 'That's it, that's my lot for today' – but a moment later it returned, sailing along the ridge line, drawing a couple of ravens for a brief spat, which made it stir its wings in a shallow beat, the first time I had seen it do this. Every other movement had been accomplished without a single movement from those massive wings. A raven's entire wing span could have fitted under a single eagle wing. It finally sank below the horizon somewhere above Mulranny.

With this confirmation of my day, I kept going, following the grassy seam of the trail. It descended towards a little stream coming off the moraine, and climbed the slope again as an orderly, diagonal transverse. A single oak flourished nearby, cradled in the throat of a narrow gully.

The trail vanished again, dispersed across the grasses, sedges and heathers of the hillside, and formed one more time as the high groove in the flank of the spur that I had noticed from the road. The wind picked up as I approached the point of maximum exposure, then eased when I got into the next valley containing the lake. Heather was suddenly deep, a rich pile of calluna offering grouse a home on this hillside, though I heard none.

Then, at the foot of a large, inclined slab, someone – once, when? – had built a five-metre section of retaining wall to support the trail – why? when you could easily step down to take a lower path? There was no practical reason that I could see. Was this some ritual impulse, to honour a processional, ceremonial track?

Barry Dalby is not sure that a mass rock ever existed at Loch an Aifrinn. Perhaps, he thinks, this was a Lughnasa site, where Tiernaur people met Ballycroy and Claggan people for a festival in the magnificent bowl of the corrie above Loch an Aifrinn.

I decided to return through the forestry, past the water treatment plant; caustic soda and sodium hypochlorite in large plastic drums at the plant. Once off the slope, I bathed my feet in a stream and ate a potato farl.

The last hour was a head-down march through forestry. A local man in a Land Cruiser gave me a lift back to the car, saving me a three-kilometre hike on a road blighted by traffic.

7th August

Weary but elated after a great evening on the river. Six fish, including a small grilse, all but one returned. The one I killed had the hook lodged in its throat and I couldn't get it out. I email Mark with a photograph of the biggest, a great lump of a sea trout, about 3lb. He replies, 'Magnificent! Congratulations as huge as that monster. The kind of evening one dreams of and rarely experiences with "the whole body", as TH would have said. Marvellous that you did.'

10th August

Mulranny. Parked at the Greenway gate, just before the old railway bridge. An Audi coming round the corner forces me to jump back, alert. I walk on to the turn at the tip of Bellacragher Bay and step off the road onto a little ramp that is marked as the start of the Lookout Hill Loop Walk. It takes me into the trees, among old birch, willow and hazel, and a deep growth of bracken. I sit down in the fly-buzz to make notes; the air is pleasantly cool, leaves rustle with a late-summer, papery dryness. Shouts and conversation from cycling families on the Greenway. Drone of a small aircraft.

This could be a start, a first step onto that great ring of ridges and summits stretching all the way from here to Bangor, a curving, discontinuous line embracing the Bellaveeny, Owenduff and Tarsaghaunmore river catchments to the west, the Owengarve to the south, and the lakes of Burrishoole to the east, along with the Owenmore to the north-east, which begins as the Altnabrocky River under Corslieve. I have approached these mountains and river valleys piecemeal, exploring them over the years from different sides, lacking the stamina or the ambition to walk the entire series in one gesture, perhaps over two days, with a break near Nephin Beg. This ring of mountains deserves to be held in the imagination as one great feature curving from Mulranny all the way to Bangor, even if it rarely tempts the walker as a single itinerary. It is best seen from the west, as the road to Ballycroy and Bangor sweeps past little inlets and estuaries. However, this distant line of uplands can be known only imperfectly to the driver of a car; its true contours must be discovered on foot, following old paths such as the Bangor Trail.

Having left the trees, I climb a staircase of rocks and roots, following pencil-black posts of recycled plastic marking the trail. A lizard scuttles away from the path into grassy undergrowth. Little streams bleed and glitter in open areas beside bog myrtle; the sound of water is a gift in this drought; it is the memory of the mountain, longer than ours. Heat is already impacting, so I make for the shade of a gorse bush, to take stock. The streeling whinny of a gull echoes from the bay, and a gossip of stonechats holds forth from the gorse. Once I leave the shade for the top of the ridge there will be no relief until the first of two bog lakes, Loch Creag a' Duileasc, two kilometres farther on.

At the first top, I turn and linger over the view of Mulranny, now a budding riviera of restaurants and modernist housing. An enamelling of cars is glinting above the beach, while at Murrevagh there's a slow-motion pulse of white foam at the edge of a corrugation of waves. The breeze is freshening in the sun, my map promises bog and bog lakes, so I pick up my bag and continue, turning my back on the holiday glamour of the resort.

Swallow chitter – they are hunting flies up here. Raven pronk, raven roll. I must keep going, I have not yet got away from traffic noise rising from the road below.

Irregularities of the undulating uplands coloured by purple moor grass, now living up to its name, with yellow-green dabs of deer sedge, and bleached stems of black bog rush. Five goats on the horizon turn and skitter across the ridge line. These goats, with some of the oldest genetic legacy anywhere in Ireland, are now on the hill of Howth, controlling the spread of gorse. Fame, of a kind.

I check the map: my lake is much farther away than I would like; progress today is slow, of the kind that maddened the colonial walkers: Stewart, Matthiessen, Thesiger, Thubron.

Goats again, twenty-three of them, some lying down, only their horns showing above the pelt of molinia. They see me and surge away, dropping out of sight – no allowance made for my photographer's needs: panoramas, veteran long-haired goats on crags, dominating the landscape.

At Loch Creag a' Duileasc, twelve swallows coming to snatch a drink of water from the shimmer; blue damselflies and larger hawkers exploring the margin. A hawker dives into the growth, buzzes frantically, then rises up, attached to another in a courtship tussle, and they fly off. I check the lake bottom: stony, three feet deep at the margin, and decide it's right for a swim. Refreshed, I walk on to the next, stonier lake, Glenamadda Lough. On bare peat, something bleached, which I take to be an antler, but it's a fragment of branch from an old Scots pine. When I pick it up and stir it, it's pliable and bendy, as it was when the breezes pushed it this way and that several thousand years ago when it was a living thing. This branch is coeval with the very first inhabitants of this island. Putting it back where I found it, it resembles a stick figure, whom I call 'Bendy', for his resilience and pliability across millennia.

The rocks here are schist and quartzite, with glinting mica and occasional bands of quartz. A rock near the lake appeared to be streaked with guano, but when I approached, it turned out to be quartz banding.

12th August

The end of a warm week, which allowed John to bale hay in the field next to the house. A large gathering of house martins (sixty-plus) with some swallows in the sky around the house. They regularly flew up into a cloud when a sparrowhawk (the same juvenile each time?) crossed below the house. The sparrowhawk has been here every day lately, and seems to sit in the trees near Gerry's place. Also, a churring whitethroat in the thick, brambly corner, where they may have bred.

15th August

With Chris on the river. Rain the previous day, the river in excellent order, although sunny spells made sea trout unlikely. Chris hooked and lost a grilse in the turn pool just above the footbridge. Then we fished the long run below Casadh na Leice, each of us hooking and losing a grilse. I also hit a sea trout briefly. A long, exhausting and fruitless day.

   A spotted flycatcher in the pine spinney beside the gate.

17th August

Moderate flood on the river. 16:00-21:00. Upstream. First fish: 1lb 6oz, foul-hooked near the vent. Two others returned: about 8oz and 1lb. Rained for about 15 mins. A beautiful, classic day. Golden slopes in the evening sun; heather in its prime. I struck and lost two other sea trout.

19th August

Layers of low mist in the hollows; clear conditions and blue sky above as the sun strikes more and more of the landscape; warm already; a heavy, glistening dew. This morning's instinct is to go straight to the top of the drumlin and pay homage to the bright blue air. A few starlings have already started to forage in the pasture, but the world up here is still intact and pristine, as I follow the north side of the fence that runs up towards the fort. A sky lark detonates from the grass and glides off towards the fort, warbling briefly; then another. I decide to search for more sky larks and dislodge a third, then a fourth in the next field along, on the ridge above John and Sandrine's house. None of these birds, at this time of year, is inclined to lift more than a couple of feet above the ground before settling again in the grass. Their song is over, and they are probably moulting. As I come back down along the same fence I avoid wandering over the pasture and so do not disturb them. Hope stores these birds for the new year: their song on bright days in late winter is one of the first signs of happier times to come.

23rd August

With Chris at Srahduggaun. He had two grilse, 2½lb and 4lb by lunchtime. He left. I went up the way and got a red fish, 4lb, returned, and a sea trout, about 1½lb, returned. After a stop at the Blue Lodge for a snack, I went down and got a 5lb salmon and a 3lb sea trout (returned) at the big pool. The sea trout took a red-arsed green peter, just as the sun had sunk low enough to put the water in shadow. There were several fish, the surface trembled with them.

24th August

Went to the river when I could have stayed at home finalising the typescript of which this journal entry might be part. There will be other days later for work at the desk, I tell myself.

I hooked and lost a nice sea trout at the junction with the little stream, which we crossed on Monday carrying expensive camera equipment. Nothing after that, the main spate has run down, but there's still a good flow. The trout just aren't 'on'.

Sitting now in the remains of an old booley hut on the srah

below Casadh na Leice, writing. I mostly rush through here, urgently, taking no time with anything other than the fishing obsession (would I be here otherwise?). No midges today in an intermittent breeze, so there is time.

Booley time. Boredom of the young lad sent up here to look after cattle, confined here for days when he could be adventuring in a boat at Dooreel or Fahy. Maybe he'd be tempted to Bangor, two hours away, where his sweetheart lives, but he'd be recognised and would get into trouble for deserting his care. Pastoral boredom, a space for stories, for dreams of love. What instrument is here to accompany a song? A ram's horn?

28th August

Sea eagle at Lough Furnace.

This evening I watch swallows from my study. They are gathering for migration, and I always feel that I should be leaving as well.

29th August

Went up the river in low water. A covey of five grouse at the pool beyond the fork at the old cattle pen. A 1lb sea trout on a small invicta. Signs of poaching at Casadh na Leice – depressing, as that pool should be full of salmon now.

30th August

Letterkeen: the Bothy Loop.

What's that on the track?
Could it be a fox's scat?
No – a butterfly!

A jay at the bothy. Tender new shoots on larch.

September

4th September

The new cones on spruce trees glow yellow in the sun, like small bananas.

11th September

Grey cloud shifting steadily south, hiding the top of Corslieve; the brow of Tamlesheffaun visible. Maumykelly and the rump of Corslieve dark, almost black; the nearer ridge of Cruach na gCapall brighter, the brown of unrefined sugar; God-beams sweeping the ridge to Tamlesheffaun, lighting the slopes yellow-green. A tear overhead shows blue; cloud openings are a bright, lit white, then heal over again to a softer light of overcast conditions. The sun blazes through a hole in the sky, then sinks again in the cloud pool.

What is the hummadruz of this place? Wind skidding off stone, rubbing the fur of the land – heather stalks, sedge blades, grass seed-heads.

Unveiling the Sun

12th September

I park at Paude's house and set out to climb Corslieve with Ged. It is several years since I was on the mountain, during the fieldwork for my book *Eagle Country* in 2016. Today I have said to Ged that I'd like to take in the southern shoulder known as Tamlesheffaun and return through the Glann, along the Bangor Trail.

There has been building activity where the Bangor Trail crosses the Tarsaghaunmore River: a new suspension bridge still looks incongruously formal in this wild setting, more like an art installation than a convenience for walkers. The old stone bothy nearby is in the process of being restored and the place is littered with builder's equipment. The ground is also scarred by the passage of quad bikes and heavy machinery. Wherever the hand of man has been in these places, before dereliction and overgrowth do their work to heal and soften, the ugliness is heartbreaking.

We cross the footbridge and head directly for the flank of the mountain; this straight line takes us onto a low intervening ridge, where we get a view of the river meandering across the bog. I spot a grouse in the heather below us and call softly to Ged, who is as pleased as I am with this discovery. The bird runs off, and is then overtaken by another that flies into deep growth ahead of it. We are pleased to have seen grouse here, just beside a depression where a degree of shelter has allowed heather to grow tall, affording cover to the birds.

The northern ridge of Corslieve forms a rump just south of the pass at Maumykelly; the western face of this rump is marked by scree and some exposed rock, and looks almost sheer from a distance, but as we approach it leans away and invites us to climb. To get there, we have to cross the Abhainn Gharbh (rough stream) running out of Glendeegan, the valley running along Corslieve's western flank. This river's rocky sequence of pools and short cascades is picturesque, with rowan and deep heather flourishing along its steep sides. Before we wade across, Ged hands me a walking pole for support, and I am grateful for this gesture from my companion, who is a licensed guide.

It takes about an hour to climb from the river to the top of the ridge. The Tarsaghaunmore diminishes to a textbook river winding across its flood plain. The scree we cross is bleached and dry, like clinkers. As we approach the top, the wind picks up and we have a strong breeze in our faces when we stop to eat a sandwich and survey the country to the north. This vast area, which Robert Lloyd Praeger, writing in 1937, found 'almost frightening in its isolation', is now marked by decades of alteration. Large areas of flow country screened by conifers, abandoned peat workings from the days of power generation at Bellacorick, a feral scrub of lodgepole pines on the same cutaway, and groves of wind turbines around Lough Dahybaun, Dáithí Bán's traditional burial place. An earlier generation of wind turbines, which I first saw many years ago when exploring this ground with my brother Liam, is now dwarfed by new aircraft-sized installations; and Ged tells me that more are planned. 'Do you think they should have demolished the cooling tower at Bellacorick?' he asks me. I tell him that I was sad to see it go, it was an elegant piece of engineering.

The breeze has chilled us, so we push on towards the summit. The cairn appears more quickly than I expected: suddenly it's there on the skyline, a heap of stones among the stones of this bare, exposed place. Somewhere, on the slope we are crossing, is a rock shaped very like an armchair, which I came across on a climb with a student many years ago. I instinctively called it Dáithí Bán's chair, and think of it today, but can't locate it this time.

Even though the summit is a modest 721 metres, it is not a place I have ever lingered. The sheer corrie walls on the eastern side are very close and induce a kind of giddiness. The inert water of Lough Adanacleveen, 'the cyclops eye', glimmers with abstraction, saying, 'these waters are too cold and dark to sustain life, and you don't belong here either. This is no place for you.'

In this alienating place, it is all the more extraordinary to notice the ruins of some kind of enclosure (and possibly a hut?) just south of the cairn, where some ritual or vigil was observed in ancient times. (According to Michael Gibbons, the enclosure probably predates the cairn.) While I understand the impulse that brought people here to build structures and perform rituals, there is more than time separating me from them and their capacity for endurance.

Ged and I observe the brief rituals of our own era: a couple of photographs of each other, with the county flag. (Mayo has lost another All-Ireland, so I have not brought my small replica of the Ardagh chalice, and can't lift it in triumph.) Then we carry on towards the shoulder at Tamlesheffaun.

Meadow pipits are still here: a small flock scatters and drifts briefly before settling again. There are swallows flying close by along the rim of the corrie; these birds are not filing through on migration but are feeding on the drift of insects being pushed up to the top of the mountain by updraught. The screeching peregrines that patrol the walls of these east-facing corries during the summer do not appear: their mountain season is over.

As the spur of the mountain turns west, forming a hook of which the main mountain is the shaft, a great view opens up of the Owenduff catchment with its glinting bog lakes, like smithereens of silver on brown velvet. It is the finest stretch of territory, to my mind, on this side of the Nephins, with an appealing emptiness that has never been diminished by forestry, unlike the bogs to the east. It is crossed, however, by a few tracks, the Bangor Trail under us, and a couple of other routes – 'traces' in local parlance – that are now rarely used, but which survive on Barry Dalby's recent map of Wild Nephin. Once or twice a year, perhaps, a walker or keen angler will cross the bog along one of these seams. Ged and I look out across the valley bottom, thinking of these routes, and of other days that could be devoted to exploring them. We also have a desire to commemorate the people for whom these old ways were part of daily life.

A lark flies up from the grass on Tamlesheffaun and chirbles briefly, one of the last gestures of a summer now drawing to a close. An open lochán here strikes us as a novelty, an infinity pool with views of Achill and the Mullet Peninsula. We walk north with the ridge, towards a depression which we name Mám a' Thóin, the Pass of the Arse, because of its resemblance to a pair of buttocks. The deep valley of Glendeegan is now between us and the stony bulk of Corslieve. Then we come off the ridge and drop down into the next valley, known locally as the Glann. The lower part of this wide bowl is clothed with the knee-deep sibilance of molinia, which we winnow with our strides. We follow a few loops of a small stream to get back to the Bangor Trail.

18th September

The weather has settled at last. A clear sky over Lough Feeagh is a song-thrush-egg blue above the horizon, darkening to a deeper azure in the dome of the heavens.

With Eleanor and Miguel and then Jessica at Currane rocks. The sea has settled to a slow thrum as it fills in the sunlight. A juvenile wheatear flits about on the sandstone overhang. Skylarks on the clifftop not inclined to rise, but still chirbling contentedly – autumn is not going to drive them off today.

Eleanor tottered across rounded sandstone boulders to get to the water, some of them draped in bright green, treacherous weed; on her way back out, she elected to crawl and clamber like some sea creature who is not well suited to land – which is the case for her as she finds relief in the water for occasional aches and pains.

We went back to the steps to rendezvous with Jessica. John and Angela Davitt were there, just back from Greece. John reads Adam Nicolson's *Why Homer Matters* every year and tells me it's essential reading. I take note.

William Maire, I tell him, caught lots of mackerel at Mulranny a fortnight ago. When he and JP went back the following evening to get more, the harvest was meagre. JP had only seven. Shoals of mackerel move about, I say. 'Very Homeric,' says John. He must have in mind the vigorous, congregating multitudes of Trojan and Greek warriors with their glinting armour, as mackerel shimmer in untold multitudes in Clew Bay. I like that. I saw the glitter of the sea today and thought of some noble and heroic tale that could be keyed on that note of immensity.

Jessica saw a sea eagle at Mulranny in a mob of corvids. The same bird (?) was reported earlier in the week from Glennamong.

19th September

What has a great lump of quartzite out there in the cold darkness got to do with me?

20th September

A halcyon day at Currane. We swam at the steps at low tide, then moved farther west to the arch, where I swam alone. I thought of Praeger and MacNeill swimming off rocks on the Antrim coast as young men – fearless, yet assessing the conditions, grabbing rock ledges to get out of the water before the backwash dragged them in again. Late-nineteenth-century exuberance and daring before the nationalist culture of the mid-twentieth tried to extinguish confidence and vitality.

The sea was calm, with very little swell. No boats of any kind on the vast expanse of Clew Bay. Ridges of Croagh Patrick and the Sheeffrys blending into a milky, soft distance. We sat on the rocks, spellbound. Some dream of privilege had come true for a few days, turning our Atlantic coast into a Côte d'Azur.

As Jessica read her novel, the lines of Yeats's 'Sailing to Byzantium' came to mind: 'the salmon falls, the mackerel crowded seas'. Everything was set at a distance on that sheet of calm, inviting water, like the life WB contemplated from a distance in that poem. The Côte d'Azur, too, became his vantage point late in life. It came to Currane for a few days this week.

21st September

Cloud is down on the mountains as I drive north, on what begins to feel like a commute. The county flags are stretched out by a brisk westerly all along the road. Tourists are still about, like the swallows, but there's a sense that their time is coming to an end.

A couple of kilometres before Ballycroy, I reverse into a gateway, turning the car towards the mountains, and take stock. All the higher summits are dissolved in grey cloud; the nearer hills have dark, emphatic shapes defining them neatly against the foggy banks in the distance. Lodgepole pine plantation is a deep carpet of bottle green thrown across the middle distance. The bog around me is a khaki pelt with lines of pale fence posts. Seed heads of molinia, with their heavy crop, register the pull of Atlantic wind in their curved inclinations, while a scattering of lark notes draws warmth – still – from the autumn land.

The N59 is neatly marked, recently resurfaced; everything this morning seems finite and measured, like the tallies of arable growers after harvest. Sitting in the car like this, I am in control;

it might be different when I start walking. I must try.

Paude is standing at the corner of his house at Tarsaghaun when I arrive, with his usual air of having expected me. As mist and drizzle close in, we stand in the shelter of a derelict old van to chat. He tells me about a few salmon that have run up the river and of dark sea trout; there are no fresh fish following the earlier flood last week. The deer rut hasn't started yet, but there is a small herd in the forestry; he has found several sets of antlers over the years. When I mention my intention to walk to the top of Slieve Alp, he tells me that there was a trap at the summit cairn years ago, 'to catch hawks'. Then the drizzle eases, and, after various assessments of the weather, I set out.

Another pulse of drizzle forces me into the shelter of a gorse bush beside the stream. A grey wagtail hunts for insects along the stones at the water's edge, then flies away upstream with another, perhaps its mate for this season.

Then I wade across the river, keeping a careful eye on the rim of my wellington boots. While I have walked along this river many times during floods, this is one of the rare occasions that I have crossed to the other side, and the first time that I leave the bright succession of pools and streams for the open bog. Within a few hundred metres, the apparent monotony of this landscape gives way to variety in the terrain: a vein of rushes and scabious at the start of a small watercourse; a hollow where shelter gives heather a chance to grow tall and lush; the furrows from the passage of a farmer's quad bike. Some way off, I see a thick fleece on the ground, and think it might be a dead sheep, but the animal stands up when I get close: I notice that its eyes are opaque, milky, and I realise that this animal is blind. It doesn't bleat or show any sign of distress and just stands there, alert to my presence. A lost creature in such a place strikes me forcefully as the epitome of loneliness. I have heard stories of hooded crows attacking the eyes of weakened sheep, even perching on their horns to bring them down.

A little farther on, another visible, dark seam in the bog expands to become the bank of a shallow lake with a tiny island where the vegetation is never grazed. As you cross flat terrain, these bog lakes are often invisible until you get to within fewer than a hundred yards: lonely, bog-locked surfaces of glitter ringed by peat banks just a couple of feet high.

Pipits and larks fly up from the short heather. One skylark is startled by my approach. A red grouse sounds its churring note somewhere in the distance. Then, a series of calls alerts me to a female merlin chasing a lark high in the air, as if this were a contest over a territory of sky, rather than a creature's flight for its life. The lark jinks and surges above the merlin, then dives suddenly to the ground, where the merlin misses it, and flies off to the south. I have not seen this falcon here for years, and am grateful for this reward after only half an hour's walk away from the river.

The ground rises slightly above the merlin lake, then crosses a broad, flat shelf before continuing to rise more steeply towards Slieve Alp. Mist is rolling in again, obscuring the top of the hill, so I head for a large boulder, where I take some time. The fox has been here: I kick away a fresh piece of fox turd before sitting down, with a ground sheet for extra shelter. My back is to the hill; the bog I have just crossed is my vista: brown, with tints of ginger, even in the driech, overcast conditions. The distance to the south is comprised of bands of grey, until all colour and shape are lost in mist.

I half expect an eagle or harrier to materialise out of these conditions, but none shows. When the drizzle arrives again in denser swathes, I decide to abandon today's destination and go back. The wettest section of the bog is also at its most colourful now: intense red sundews; swollen-grape bundles of blossom at the tips of cross-leaved heath; ling in flower; salmon-pink and orange flames of bog asphodel gone to seed; yellowing tips of molinia and beaked sedge, the leaves of molinia now at their darkest; cottongrass an intense, fiery chestnut; wine-red, yellow, and green sphagnum, the biggest clumps like heaps of an oriental spice; heraldic tormentil leaves; pale matrixes of stag's horn moss. And a tiny pale butterwort in flower, above its short rosette of sticky, insectivorous leaves. Some animal – the fox? – has been rooting into the ground for food, leaving small cup shapes in the vegetation: I find a little nest of four carder bees in one of them. They are damp and drowsy, as if they had been bingeing on this year's 'mellow fruitfulness'.

My binoculars find a young stag, calmly grazing along the forestry edge in mid-afternoon.

By the time I get back to the river, another clearance has uncovered the top of the hill: I did not wait long enough and have missed today's opportunity – O me of little faith!

Paude has been clearing thistles and burdock in the field next to his house with a curious billhook: the blade is very broad, more like a medieval weapon of war than a farmer's tool. He is very glad to hear about the missing sheep, which is one of this year's ewe lambs, and will go out to collect it.

24th September

Fished the river from 18:00 to dusk. A huge flood two days earlier gone well down. No sea trout, although conditions nice. No sign of salmon either.

Chris reports an excellent run of salmon on the Owenmore with this week's floods. This year's run of sea trout was late July, early August. September has been warm, without much rain, but today's drizzle presages a change. Next week the wind will swing westerly and the Atlantic low pressure will pile in, with wind and rain. Drizzle all day today, with no chance of a clearance.

I read Nan Shepherd's *The Living Mountain* again this week, for the third or fourth time. Robert Macfarlane emphasises what a slim volume it is, which sets me thinking that Shepherd could have written a longer book, covering the territory in much the same way that Tim Robinson extended his narrative across Aran and Connemara. She must have heard many stories from the old folk, such as Big Mary, the gamekeeper's wife, who preferred the rough life outdoors to the wifely duties of 'housecraft'. She could also have assembled a more objective account of the Cairngorms, if only she were not impatient with textbooks: the descriptions in the geography books, she declares at the outset, are 'a pallid simulacrum of their reality': and so she is drawn deeper, to explore the essence of the Cairngorms, into 'a reality of the mind'.

So many of her formulations jump off the page, like aphorisms breaking free of the narrative. 'Place and a mind may interpenetrate till the nature of both is altered.' [8] 'It is worth ascending unexciting heights if for nothing else than to see the big ones from nearer their own level.' [19] 'Simply to look on anything, such as a mountain, with the love that penetrates its essence, is to widen the domain of being in the vastness of non-being.' [102] 'The thing to be known grows with the knowing.' [108]

Some mountains come pre-packaged, with their own identities and stories (the Reek, Nephin), while others have to be invented or reimagined, especially where the communities that used to know them are now extinct or declining. When Corslieve is lost in mist, as it will be today, it is also lost in 'the vastness of non-being', and that constitutes its margin of terror. To redeem it from that awesome vastness might be worth the attempt. There is not enough in the archive to constitute a story, only to provide a few springboards or cues; the walker must do the rest, with an occasional companion, if not alone.

Unveiling the Sun

In the drizzling mist, there is nothing in the distance for the eye, but when you turn to nearer things, there is a great deal of interest. There is never more variety and colour in the vegetation than at this time of year, when flowers, fruition and the first fadings of autumn are all combined. In these damp, overcast conditions, the glare of sunlight is removed and the colours have a greater intensity, similar to the vivid intensity of the landscape in the evening just after sunset. This makes for the great appeal of autumn and winter walking, especially when there is no distraction from the blue glare of sky overhead, and from the allure of higher summits and ridges.

I decide to make for the plantation at Tarsaghaun, to revisit Loch Hughie Phaitín, a lake that I had glimpsed years ago but not explored properly. In Paude's account, wild geese visited here in the old days, which must have been before the forestry was planted. He tells me that he sees the heron there regularly, hunting for eels. To get there, you go into the forestry near 'the white scraws'.

A hind is grazing at the edge of trees as I tramp across the bog, looking for whatever is meant by those white scraws; then it moves off into cover. I flounder through deep molinia at the edge of a drain to reach a firebreak; fifty metres ahead is the first patch of open water, a small lochán annotated with stalks of bog bean and pipewort. Then I glimpse the lake away to my right, beyond a failing stand of lodgepole.

I sit for an hour at the edge of the trees, to eat a sandwich and bear witness to this lonely body of water. The foresters left a broad margin all the way around, so the pines stand back from the lake at a distance of between twenty and fifty metres. Ling heather is deep around the open margin, with a few rhododendrons and some naturally seeded conifers. A dabchick pair are calling and squabbling between dives for food, and there's a single female teal feeding in a narrow circle. Sedges and rushes rooted on the bed of this shallow lake are showing across much of the surface. My attachment to this place reminds me of the obscure child in one of Wordsworth's Lucy poems:

She dwelt among the untrodden ways
Beside the springs of Dove,
A maid whom there were none to praise
And very few to love.

    The heron is not here today; the forest stirred by a breeze sounds like a softly foaming wave along the seashore, with fainter pin-holes of bird calls. The hind I saw earlier is unlikely to venture out towards the lake, knowing that I am here.

    When I stand up to take a photograph of the lake, the teal rises and flies off briefly before settling again: a first lesson in intrusiveness. Deer have made a narrow track between the lake and the forest, which I follow for convenience. There's a heap of boulders with an otter's signature just off the northern shore, marking some obscure enterprise many years ago.

    As this lake is surrounded by open bog and forest, it has scarcely any catchment; only the heaviest, most sustained rain causes it to spill over into the little outlet at the far southern end. My friend Jean-Pierre Maire constantly marvels at the instinct of sea trout, which will take every opportunity to run up little streams, even into lakes that may be cut off for many months when the spate subsides. Could some of them be here, I wonder? A few fish are making occasional surges near the surface, but there are no signs of trout rising for a fly, or jumping clear. The map shows a little fiodán connecting this lake to the Tarsaghaunmore River, but as I cross it I discover little more than a muddy seam among tufts of molinia. Loch Hughie Phaitín is essentially a large bog lochán, without that vital connection to a river and the sea which gives seasonal drama to larger lakes, with runs of silver sea trout.

I sit again at the forest edge, overlooking the narrow, southern end, watching the wind playing on the tantalising surface. Black darter dragonflies lift from the deep grass; the dabchick entertains me for a while among the tremors of these moving, invisible fish. Then a high-pitched raptor call rises from the far side, and a few flickers of movement, swift-like, glimpsed above the pines – the bird dashes across the forest edge and alights on a branch twenty feet up. The under-tail coverts show brilliantly white, so I am haunted briefly by an old yearning, to find a goshawk here. Then the bird takes to the air again and leaves – a female sparrowhawk annoyed at this rare human intruder into its territory.

A dark butterfly settles on the ling ahead of me and opens its wings. This red admiral seems fresher, more vivid than any I have seen before on buddleia in suburban gardens; the circle of orange on black, and the clear white marbling seem too glamorous for this place and I decide it must be a recent migrant, drifted here on warm southerlies.

The hind is back again in the same place as before, grazing near the fence line as I emerge from the trees; its response to my appearance is cautious, not terrified: I admire this fine animal as it crosses my sight again on its way back to cover.

My track back to the road is more toilsome than before because I take a line slightly adrift of my outward route and am deep in tussocks of molinia for a while. The blades of this grass still have their rich summer colours of green and purple, but by late winter when the cold season has done its work, these tussocks will be completely bleached out, in stark contrast to the darker heathers and sedges. I have, quite literally, stumbled into the meaning of the placename: 'the white scraws'.

27th September

Tall towers and sprays of cumulus are arriving from the Atlantic with blue sky behind them, so that the mountains, ridges and lower ground are constantly passing from shade to light and back again. These are excellent conditions for revealing the volume and structure of mountains. A peak may be in shadow while the lower ridge of a corrie is prominent in full light against the dull backdrop; yet another ridge in front of it is also in shadow, so that the corrie ridge is highlighted on its own, in considerable detail.

The peak of Corslieve, seen from the south at Letterkeen, usually just an obscure grey shoulder glimpsed behind Nephin Beg, now takes on a depth and structure of its own. The summit and its cairn are in silhouette, but with binoculars I can see the bright green rim of Coire Leachta curving towards me like a blade. The walls of the same corrie under the summit are covered in dark striations.

When the forecast rain does eventually come, this play of light and shadow is overwhelmed; the mountains settle back to a grey two-dimensional existence – but for one difference: you have understood something of their proportions.

30th September

Showery in the morning, clearance in the afternoon, blustery from the west. Got to the river by four, walked upstream as far as Casadh na Leice. Caught a dark sea trout (14oz) in the stomach pool.

As I fished one of the flats in the approaching darkness, a low cloud brought a nasty squall and darkened the scene even further. The pool was choppy, the water the colour of ink with a silvery sheen on the surface, the landscape as bleak as can be at this latitude. The imagination needs no more than this to grasp the Styx and the glooms of the underworld.

Paddy's house is now deserted, leaving two homes in the glen. People were never meant for these places, only grouse, deer, fish and eagles.

October

2nd October

This morning was the crows' acorn dance above the oaks in the garden. The sky was bright blue, and wind was driven briskly from the south, lifting them up the slope, keeping them airborne. There were about a dozen rooks at one time, with a few jackdaws, and occasionally a magpie. The rooks and jackdaws, in twos and threes, performed playful jousts around the crowns of the oaks, lunging at each other, twisting and climbing, spinning suddenly, all this apparently from a surplus of energy on an exuberant morning of wind and light. The rooks' legs hung down like the talons of eagles before they land, but these birds were taken up with airborne frolics, and didn't come down.

The acorns are ready – I noticed the full fruit just the other day – and the crows have been coming down to them, but this morning's performance was a kind of festival marking this harvest, perhaps a favourite crop of the corvid year, and both weather and conditions provided the right occasion. Something in rook memory might be telling them that this site will be a rookery of the future (it will not), so their performance could be stirred by the breeding impulse as well.

Wind rushing through the trees this morning was also the energy of the crows rounding off their year before the drudgery of their winter routines.

3rd October

It was late when I got away (echoes of Philip Larkin). Grey cloud over the mountains had smothered what little light there was left in a low sun to the west. Leaves on sycamores and alders were dark and crisp, if they had not fallen; ash were bright yellow in the gloom.

My dream of winter was well lit, a space of frost and light and – perhaps – snow, with the shores of Lough Feeagh ringing with the calls of greenshank; this evening was a dark, sullen prequel. Wind was tousling the bushes by the roadside and the lake water was rough in the little bays, cancelling any hope of an otter steering through the meniscus. There was colour in this landscape, I knew, but my urgent drive sped past the browns and khaki shades that deserved closer examination.

I wanted to get to Letterkeen to listen for rutting stags. Hunters were to arrive in a few days at Ballycroy to the west to hunt them; the *Irish Times* had just published a front-page photograph of a rutting deer in the Phoenix Park. The time had come, winter was beginning, and I wanted to witness it.

The road to Letterkeen leads past Lough Feeagh, under Crimlin Hill, along the flat plain formed by the river valley, the great srah – Shramore. In its upper reaches, this valley is choked with rhododendron, and the road is crowded on each side with walls of the heavily pruned shrub. Hills and mountains of the

Nephin Beg range rise on either side as you move among them, 'a romantick appearance', said Richard Pococke approvingly when he travelled through here in 1752, possibly the first gentleman tourist ever to do so. Groups of sauntering sheep were moving ahead of the car as I drove into the forest, most of them little blackfaces, which thrive in this wild terrain.

In recent years, I had seen very few signs of deer at the southern end of the range: a line of hoofprints on a forestry track in Glennamong, north-west of Lough Feeagh, and a few tracks along a plantation edge at Loch na mBarún were the only indications that they had spread this far. Several years ago, a friend and I heard several at Keenagh, farther north, one calm October evening: their dry, vaulted braying still echoed with me, and I thought it would be easy to locate if any animals were present at Letterkeen.

Instead of going to the bothy, now renamed the Robert Lloyd Praeger Centre, I drove straight on, along the Nephin drive, and parked at a layby where the managers of the Wild Nephin area had put a panorama photograph of the range. The view was impressive: the long ridge of Correen More, the huge recumbent mass of Nephin Beg with the vast hollow of Coire na gCapall on its southern flank, and, briefly appearing in the distance, just the grey shoulder of a ridge off Corslieve, the highest and least visited peak of all. Forestry was still a dominant feature of this landscape, but there were glinting river bends and open moorland flats to contrast with the encroachment of these newcomers. The haphazard patchwork was indeed a candidate for wilderness, a kind of Irish domestication of Western American conifer forest, minus wolves and bears.

This evening there were no animal sounds: only the rustling, whispering of wind-rushes through conifer needles, which Rob Macfarlane calls 'psithurism', from a Greek word meaning 'whispering'.

This whispering was replete with cold at that height, so I went back to the car and sat for a while with the window open. Nothing echoed from the young larch and spruce plantations below me, or from the mature stands in the distance. I imagined cantering stags and the clash of antlers in some distant place, perhaps beside the forestry at Bellaveeny or Tarsaghaun, but none were here, so I turned the car and came down the track to a more sheltered position. Instead of the gusting psithurism of young spruce, I heard a pair of jousting robins at evensong, and a raven croaking through the fading light.

When I drove on, with full headlights, a few chaffinches and thrushes, startled by the glare, did snipe-dives across the beams. Then these were upstaged by whirring patrols of pipistrelles along the tree edges lining the road. By now trees and hills were silhouettes against the dregs of leaden light in the sky overhead. Then the road arrived at the lakeshore, where waves were foaming on the stones, working away; the water seemed dark and inert as shape and space were being swallowed by night, but I knew that salmon were lodged there in numbers, waiting for the shortest days when they would spawn.

Winter was coming – not the vigil of darkness it might seem, but a special theatre of light and colour, which I looked forward to. As I turned around the last arm of Lough Feeagh before leaving the valley, a single white moth, pure and bright, glinted for an instant in the headlights.

7th October

Corslieve drains mostly into two catchments: almost all the rainwater off the western flank runs into the Tarsaghaunmore River, which then joins the Owenduff on its westward journey into Blacksod Bay; rainfall on the eastern side runs mostly north into the Altnabrocky River and the Andrews Stream, two tributaries of the Owenmore, which also flows west and enters the Blacksod basin. Therefore the entire watershed of Corslieve is gathered on a westward journey; none of it flows south into the Burrishoole catchment, or east into the Deel River and Lough Conn.

Rain has been sweeping in for days on warm southerlies. I want to see the mountain again, or at least see the water that runs from the mountain, so I go back to Tarsaghaun More.

Today's mild, almost tropical weather is not good for scenery; the hills and mountains are undistinguished, draped in mist, or come briefly into focus in an interval of drizzle as grey zones of distant ridges. A few vertical white streaks on the hillsides mark the cascades in spate, like the waterfall at Scardaun, a distant, silent signature of water's power.

Paude emerges from his house when he hears the dog barking at my arrival. He has retrieved the blind sheep; it's recovering its sight, he tells me. Sheep with diseased eyes can stumble into bog locháns, where the still water is silent; they avoid rivers and lakeshores, where water noise alerts them to danger.

I set out upstream in fine drizzle. The river in spate is a shoaling avenue of trembling, truculent water. The surface is a steely grey, while in places the current meets large rocks and rears up in a wave breaking against the flow; at every instant these glassy crests are flung up from the main current, showing the brown colour of rock candy, but the foam at the crest of the surge is almost white.

The stream is spread to a wide avenue of running water, with blustery air snatching drops from the foaming crests or scuffing the surface with grey. Much of this water is too fast for an angler's fly; but in a few places there are slower eddies and currents off the main flow where running fish could rest. I search for these with an alert, hunter's eye.

The builders have not yet finished at the bothy, but the floor is neatly tiled with clean Indian sandstone; I leave my rucksack in a corner and continue on, crossing the footbridge to one of my favourite spots.

The second pool above the footbridge is a deep belly in the river. The water here twists upwards in the centre of the stream, upwelling strongly, creating conditions that are not favoured by salmon – they prefer a steady, even current. On the far side, however, where the current is weaker, and the flow smoother, I notice a run that looks ideal for a salmon to lie in or pause on its way upstream to the spawning beds. Of all the places, this is where my eye is drawn; then, right on cue, a salmon shows briefly, its head and back clear of the surface for an instant. This moment is enough to bring the entire river to life. I am mesmerised, and keep my eye on the same spot for several minutes. Within a quarter of an hour, the fish shows again, this time a brief snout emerging above the surface. Anglers will speculate about why migrating fish do this. My guess is that they get a glimpse of their surroundings, in conditions where the water itself is too agitated to give them clear horizons.

The sight of a salmon in this spate river is thrilling. In low water in summer, there are not many places where they can hide, so they are vulnerable, but now, at winter levels, the water is to their advantage; the river is a greater thing with many flows and pools keeping them from rods and nets. The angling season is officially over, and now the dark, cold time is approaching when the salmon's spawning urge kicks in.

From my perspective, the river is streaming to the left; when I look up and stare at the grass on the other bank, it appears to be revolving to the right. I keep staring, telling my eye-brain that the ground is fixed, but it is still revolving, like a dizzy horizon. As I walk back to the bridge, I feel queasy, as if I have been in a boat rocked by the motion of water.

A jack merlin flies up from a flooded hollow on the srah: he arrows away, and looks not much bigger than a kingfisher; his blue mantle in these grey conditions has almost a kingfisher's intensity. Three snipe rise silently from the same plashy spot.

This weather dissolves peaks and horizons, with the added effect of eroding distinctions between heights. The entire landscape is like a stage where the curtain has been lowered to within a couple of feet of the floor and all we see are the legs of the actors.

9th October

Distances are clearing, the light has been washed by days of rain. Cloud is reluctant to leave the highest tops, but the lower slopes are a brilliancy of autumn colour.

Jess and I walk in the Bellaveeny plantation in the afternoon, our mission to see deer or hear rutting stags. The plantation is partly hidden from the main road, so you don't appreciate its size until you approach along the forestry track. It's about 1000ha, by my estimate, with much second-cycle planting of young lodgepole, but there are several veteran stands as well, acquiring character from year to year; a haven for crossbills.

The electricity network people have cut a broad swathe of young lodgepoles under the power lines to the water scheme at Loch an Aifrinn; this forms a vivid chestnut stripe parallel to the track. The sign of the Rock House Sporting Estate has its top broken off, but the 'No Hunting or Shooting' message survives.

Robins are singing at the start of their winter vigil. Many broad yellow boletus mushrooms decorate the margins; these are the fruiting bodies of large mycorrhizal networks throughout the ground, those systems that allow trees to communicate by connecting their roots, according to recent research. It is happening here.

Jess strides ahead. I'm studying the track for deer prints,

when children's voices suddenly break the solemnity of our visit. Two, three, then five children, a girl and four boys returning along the track followed by their parents. They have the self-sufficiency of a large family that doesn't need others for company, and can make their own amusement in this unfrequented place. Although their noisy play might have put paid to our chances of seeing deer this afternoon, this carefree exuberance makes me happy: there are no gaming devices in sight.

The evening glows on the hillsides. Corslieve and Tamlesheffaun are almost fully revealed in the low sun, their pied beauty of scree, peat, heather and grass like the fur of a big cat resting in dappled shade.

Larch starting to turn, showing gold in places, but not yet the bright colour that will come soon.

10th October

Another beautifully mild autumn day. A Spanish girl at the college complains that it rains a lot in Ireland – we laugh at this because there has been so little rain lately. Plenty of growth still; the only frost came briefly about two weeks ago. The ash trees are turning that lovely lemon yellow, and the sycamore on the Lodge Road is dark, dusky orange. Two nights ago I saw a woodcock at dusk, species number 68 on our list. Mice scrabbling in the attic, on cue for the season. Stonechats about the place. I cut the hawthorns along the boundary to chest height last weekend; now we have a hedge. Yellowish bells on the arbutus.

13th October

Jean-Pierre drops me off at the Owenduff, just down from Sheeaun Lodge, where a footbridge takes me across the river.

There's a herder's cottage here, and another house, now derelict, in a grove of imposing sitkas.

At first, I follow the coils of a narrow stream coming out of Gleann Cam, between the hills of Slieve Alp and Marafach. This valley would have been my approach to the Bangor Trail where it runs through the Glann, with the opportunity of seeing Fiodán a' Chailín, but I lack energy and ambition today, and instead am drawn towards Slieve Alp, which seems a simpler excursion.

On this open terrain, there's little chance of seeing rutting deer – though stags do occasionally cross the bog – but one plant has put on an autumn show that matches the season perfectly: deer grass (*Trichophorum cespitosum*) is changing from green to yellow to fiery chestnut to dark chocolate: you can see the succession on every stalk from base to tip, and this red-deer hue predominates across the valley floor and up the hillside, where it is offset perfectly by starry tufts of bleached mat grass, a sign of the years when this ground was under even more grazing pressure than now.

For a hill of 329 metres, Slieve Alp is rather grandly named, but I'm drawn to it for a view of Corslieve from its summit. A steady hike out of Gleann Cam gets me to the top of its shoulder, but the peak itself leans away from me, still almost a kilometre further on. The ground changes to a crazy paving of bleached quartzite on bare peat, with hags of vegetation standing proud, like the crests of breaking waves. If peat were solid, the profile of this ground would be a skateboarder's dream with its curved sides and white-silted hollows. On the final approach to the top, the ground changes again: deer grass has now given way to a tight sward of ling, bell heather and crowberry, couched in sphagnum and woolly fringe moss (*Racomitrium laguninosum*), that typical moss of the uplands.

What the map calls the Tower turns out to be the largest of three cairns, shallow piles of blocks that have not seen much activity for a long time. I wonder who might have built these. When, if ever, was this hill a resort of hill-walkers like myself? Or was there a much more locally focussed pattern of sheepmen marking the autumn gathering off the hills by coming up here in a festival mood to view their own landscape and swap stories of places they could see, from Achill to the Mullet, and north to the hills overlooking the Owenmore? A kind of agallamh na seanórach, or debate of the elders, when it was possible in this way only to visualise your territory before the era of maps and television?

I get up and walk a few irregular loops around the cairns, performing a kind of station of my own; the ground is marked by a formation of large, angular rocks like a defensive *chevaux-de-frise*. A large bottle nested in moss is still shining, perhaps years after being discarded here. The wind is chilly, so I retreat farther down the slope, and on the way pick a few leaves of bilberry to chew on, and satisfy some ritual need to remember Lughnasa gatherings on this, or other high places.

There's a scattering of feathers from a falcon strike: when I gather a handful and put them together in a bunch, the plumage is pale brown fringed with tawny. One morning several weeks ago, while the nest on Corslieve still had young, a peregrine falcon quartered this hillside and brought down a grouse to feed its hungry brood. A little farther on, I see droppings, perhaps left by the bird who died here. In the absence of live birds, I have to construct my own portion of grouse from a peregrine's leftovers.

This slope looks east towards the Bangor Trail and the long transverse running across the main massif towards the spur at Tamlesheffaun. Within 180 degrees of here, you can see Tarsaghaun More to the north, the ascending lines of Corslieve, and the Owenduff catchment to the south. Apart from one narrow belt of forestry beyond Maumykelly, the landscape is entirely open, in contrast to the forestry and peat workings on the eastern side. This is truly an Empty Quarter, and it takes a search with binoculars to find faint traces of people, such as the Bangor Trail itself, climbing out of the Glann. On the slope under Tamlesheffaun, two large blocks of quartz set side by side catch my eye: the trail makes a detour straight up the slope towards them and crosses a stream at that point: they are such a feature here that walkers make the extra effort to reach them.

The mountain top has withdrawn again into cloud cover, refusing to show for my camera. A few small rents of blue allow God-beams like searchlights to caress the bog with shifting pools of golden light. Silence is punctuated by sporadic raven calls and the murmur of a transatlantic flight. Waves of brightness cross the northern shoulder of Corslieve; patches of Wedgewood blue are showing through the cumulus; the Owenduff catchment at Srahduggaun is a drift of thin veils of light.

As I return across the shoulder of Slieve Alp, a single female wheatear among the rocks and heather surprises me, the warmth of its buff colour out of place here now as winter encloses the land with its grip.

This brings a different emotional reach, into my own past, with its regrets and griefs. Winter is a concentration of these feelings, when the pageantry of summer is absent. There's an increasing simplicity here; and as that simplicity is refined by these open spaces you approach the truth of your own life. As Elizabeth-Jane Burnett has said memorably, with reference to open spaces, 'You meet yourself on the moors, where the limits are all yours.' Not that you need to deliver this truth as the painful details of memoir: instead, life resolves into a feeling there might be a name for, but what that is I cannot say, only that today in the purity of this solitude there's a tide of feeling welling up. There are many more spaces among these ridges and hollows where, as I follow the explorer's need, I might uncover more of what Robert Macfarlane has called 'topographies of self', where old paths offer 'not only means of traversing space, but also ways of feeling, being and knowing.'

The vegetation softens again on the way back down into Gleann Cam. The old remains of a dead sheep puzzle me: the fleece is wrapped in a few twists of barbed wire, as if this were some contrivance to trap a fox or a raven; instead I figure out that the animal got badly snagged in a discarded length of wire and eventually died out here.

I stop one final time beside the little stream that drains the glen, with a view along a deep, narrow pool that must hold sea trout in these few weeks before spawning. The surface is rocked by slight disturbances as fish patrol this twenty-metre lane of brightness. A young stonechat pops up on a small tuft of peat on the top of the riverbank ten yards away and inspects me for a moment. This is my favourite little brown bird of remote, abandoned places. Wherever there's some deep ground cover, even in the loneliest hollow in the mountains, you'll find the stonechat holding territory. Their fidelity to such places means that severe winters can almost wipe out their populations, but stonechats recover quickly from the coastal margins, where a few survive on pickings from the shore. There are not many insectivores that can subsist in the uplands throughout the year, and none with the dapper colouring of the male stonechat. During the winter, wrens churr in the undergrowth, and meadow pipits scatter like spindrift, but the stonechat makes a stand on the slightest vantage point and repeats his *chak-whee*, *chak-whee* call to defend his mountain home. They are my emblem of humble resilience. Auden's lines from his poem 'The Wanderer' seem perfectly attuned to this occasion, where the bird becomes an emblem of a man in strange places, without any of the comforts of home:

lonely on fell as chat,
By pot-holed becks
A bird stone-haunting, an unquiet bird.

From the account of the rocky terrain, the chat the poet had in mind was probably a wheatear, which happens to be a close cousin of the stonechat; both species, one a migrant, the other a resident, have kept me company today.

15th October

Storm Ophelia. Jess and I drove to Lough Feeagh at Srahmore, and parked at the new layby and steps, to walk the Western Way, past the fairy tree. The proverbial calm before the storm. I had heard of American research on warblers, using geo-locators, demonstrating that birds had retreated south in advance of a storm, and I wondered whether our creatures could hear the approaching hurricane.

  Our outward walk was a heads-down, unobservant march. The air was thick with the fetid smell of sheep urine and droppings. We reached the road again and walked back towards the lake past the old national school and the small R.C. church. We saluted a local man with white hair and a beard, who sat on the wall of the church, smoking. The reflections of willows in the water of the old river very clear and beautiful. Many holly trees with berries along the road. Ravens flew off Crimlin and crossed Srahmore, heading north. A few woodpigeons gyred about in a gathering flock, as if they had indeed just realised that a major storm was approaching. As we neared the car, the original group of twelve had swollen to thirty-four, flying high above the oak wood.

  The lake quite still and inert, as usual; no sign of a greenshank yet. The zones of vegetation on Torc Shléibhe very distinct:

chocolate-brown at the top; yellow-green lower down where mat grass predominated; another field was the orange colour of deer grass; there were also many overlapping strips of tawny bracken. Winter colours are setting in, though the day is still mild, and the oak is just now shot through with gold.

In Lidl on the way home, a stir of people stocking up for tomorrow. Met Eireann advice is to stay indoors in the counties affected by the Red Weather Warning: Waterford, Cork, Kerry, Limerick, Clare, Galway, Mayo (this was later extended to cover the whole country).

Our perception of extreme weather is mostly of human preparations – crowds in supermarkets, traffic jams on highways, disconsolate and distressed home owners – rarely of the thing itself. We stay indoors, beside radio and TV updates. No-one, except the wind surfers, engages with the intrinsic phenomenon. The storm become a news story of avoidance and distress: it is rarely encountered in its own manifestation: cataracts, woods swaying, waves pounding a shore. My resolution for tomorrow is to observe the storm, and not be distracted by news of the storm. All this is predicated on the roof not blowing off, and of having a secure position from which to watch.

20:30 Rain pattering on the roof above the downstairs bathroom.

16th October

06:00 I woke and went to the bathroom. Then I lay in bed, listening to the wind. A few slates clicked as they vibrated; occasional buzzings told of a fascia thrumming in the air's energy. Then there were more diffuse whooshings, wind coming round the house, friction between air and concrete. Were there also, I wondered, in these surges, sounds of friction of air around a gable, meeting another rushing of air coming against it? And so the verbs become pure gerund, having no object, being just an action in itself.

Another softer sound began on the roof above me, of big drops falling, as if a cat with a thousand paws had crossed the slates and vanished. That was succeeded by a denser pattern, as if a sequence of waves had tossed a froth of small fish onto the roof repeatedly. Then, stronger still, came a beating, like sheaves of oats being struck against the top of the house as the raindrops rebounded. Last of all, after an interval, came the hum of pouring where you could not distinguish individual drops; the rain came as one continuous sound, like a crop of fruit being released down a chute into a hopper, in a single rush.

09:00 The wind is easterly, gusting to gale force, not yet a storm. The fields seem empty, as if a pitch had been prepared for some great legendary encounter; the searching eye finds sheep in the lee of the drumlins, still going about their business. The oak foliage is a surf of green shot with gold and orange, swaying and shifting in a dance it is unaccustomed to, because strong winds here are normally from the west, not the east. Like a girl who puts her hands in front of her skirt to protect her modesty, and is shocked when the breeze lifts her skirt from behind. The rage of trees keeps pace with alarming news bulletins, a blend of retrospect and anticipation, but then the agitation relents, the surf of leaves calms down, just as, in the interval between large waves, the frothy surface settles briefly. A yellow sun leaks down onto the horizon through grey cloud for a few minutes until an approaching fog of rain draws the curtain on this light.

A flock of seven whooper swans, recently arrived from Iceland, steers big wings unsteadily into the valley, looking for a lake to take their cumbersome weight.

11:15 Beyond the oaks, the hawthorn hedges are without leaves; a rich crop of haws has darkened, the fruit having dried out somewhat since August, when the red berries were flush in their bouquet of leaves.

Wind is more southerly, the tree-tops are pushing towards the house; the movement is hesitant, less strong than an hour ago, as if Aeolus were breathing in, getting ready for the next blow. A glaring column of sunlight rises to the south-west, over the Partry Mountains, glints on rooftops for a few seconds, and diminishes, as the stairway to heaven is withdrawn skyward. Air and cloud mass are now distinctly southerly.

12:30 Wind is increasing in strength. The windows upstairs facing south are now a blur, as fine rain is being blown against them and the distance darkens. The west gable window is still clear for viewing. Poplars are bare-looking, with just a thin remnant of dark, dried-up leaves. Each point is like the tip of a fly rod that has hooked a big trout, bending northwards. More rain is being flung in squalls at the window panes: the best-dressed trees (oak, beech and alder) are now toiling in distress, while their naked cousins (rowan and poplar) stand by demurely. The most beautiful apparition of all, though, in this daytime gathering, is a mature arbutus at the gate. It benefits from this realignment of perspectives. The summer's pale new growth is still fresh and luxuriant, as this is not a deciduous tree, and the creamy bells of its flowers are just appearing along its flanks. It is less distressed than the deciduous trees, and is enjoying the storm dance, shifting and wobbling its spongy mass. This female tree has not yet fruited; it is still trying to attract a male, which explains its voluptuous dance.

14:00 Rain sets in again in earnest. Hollywood rain, where directors have fire-hoses aimed at cars, streets and buildings. Jess and I sit over dinner as water streams down the windows or bounces off the walls outside. A lone mallard crossing the sky has the speed and purpose of a fighter aircraft on a sortie at the height of the Battle of Ophelia.

By the time we are drinking tea following the meal, the wind has slackened again as the rain eases. For a brief interval the hedges are almost calm. This is the moment the eye of the storm passes. Then, as I take a phone call from my son Seamus, the wind picks up again, this time from the west, its usual quarter. This is the wind we know, the one we have made provision for, planting a hedge with trees, including a line of eighteen black poplars along the western side of the garden. We have endured many fierce nights from that quarter and feel that we can cope with this as well.

Now the deluging rain from lunchtime has spread from the Moyour stream into the fields. The floodwaters are a muddy brown colour, as this spate has been so sudden, flushing out drains and ditches. Water also lies on the surface of the fields, like broad applications of grey or green.

17:00 We watch the poplars, pines and alders nodding in the gale, a sight we are well accustomed to, having sat through storms of force ten and eleven several times. If the wind doesn't increase further, we are now hopeful that the worst may be over. The oak grove, which entertained us this morning with its south-easterly dance of leaf-surf, is relatively quiet, as it lies in the lee of other plantings on the western side.

Already, it is possible to speak of this storm's legacy: drifts of sycamore leaves torn from two trees at the gate are thick and sodden, piled near the front door.

17:40 A steady westerly gale in the poplars. Rain starts again, a mizzle greying the distance.

18:30 We put on hi-viz waistcoats and go out. Roads deserted. The river a mass of brown water; hawthorns along the river are stark above their reflections on the floodwater. We walk through water near the dipper bridge; the brook out of Hazelbrook is bolting urgently away, like a guilty thing. A gloomy world. One car came up the hill past Gerry's place as we went down. A pair of bats hunted along the road in the twilight; one flew straight at Jessica and veered off at the last moment less than two feet from her face.

17th October

Skerdagh-Glenlara. 'No hunting, no training of dogs, no shooting,' says a sign on the way into the forestry. No fresh signs of deer. Clear-felling. Maybe *no* deer now.

18th October

I write overlooking Lough Feeagh. I feel despondent at yesterday's walk with Jess in Glenlara, at the dismal wreckage of clear-felling. We had previously seen deer here, including superb views of two bucks locking antlers in youthful play. The eastern side of the valley is heavily grazed. There is much more heather among the tree enclosures than on the open hillside.

On our return on foot from the end of the track, we disturbed a dipper from a small stream running in a trench between stands of clear-felling. The bird flew about in a wide arc before returning to the water-course, showing its bib, saying, 'I'm not an ordinary blackbird: this is me, and I have to get by in this scene of devastation. Would you just look at it!'

How little respect there is in dealing with the land.

The Earthshot prizes were announced last night for action on climate change and habitat destruction; today I'm back here again, surveying a melancholy scene along the lake. Now that I feel obliged to moderate my petrol consumption I can't drive off to the mountains every day to say my planetary prayers.

19th October

In the National Park between Tubbrid and the Western Way, with Ged and Thérèse's students from Achill.

Usnea on the larch is truly magnificent, as the larch turns gold, with an admixture of dark green lodgepole pine by way of contrast.

The forest very quiet again. We paused at An Mhuing Mhór. One of the students proposed being quiet for a minute. In that minute there was scarcely a sound, just the churring of a wren and tiny goldcrest notes.

Anna, from Germany, showed me a chestnut boletus mushroom. There were several, most of them over, past their best; we should have been here three weeks ago to see them in their prime. Also, a fly agaric beside the path, the first time I have seen this mushroom here.

20th October

The day has cleared after a night's rain and the mountains are free of cloud. Corslieve is smiling.

As I drive through plantation at Bellaveeny a massive bird appears at treetop height, flying away. I know it is a sea eagle, and then with binoculars I see the white tail of an adult, and a blue wing tag. The bird flies east towards Blue Lodge and then turns south, going low across the bog towards the main plantation under Loch an Aifrinn. This is news I want to share so I text a few people; I also mention it to a sheepman driving a flock along the road at Sheean. 'You'll look after them, won't you?' I say in my boyish, naïve enthusiasm. This kind of openness is more in my nature than the wary, guarded secrecy espoused by others in the conservation movement, whose empires of knowledge are built on a principle of exclusion. Apart from the exact location of nest sites, my view is to let people know, and offer them a share in the experience.

I stop for a bowl of soup at the visitors' centre and talk about this discovery. Michael Chambers tells me about other reports of buzzards and eagles, some unconfirmed; there's definitely a sense that these observations are happening more frequently outside the main strongholds in the south-west and on the Shannon. Donegal has a territorial pair, there are also birds on the Erne system in Fermanagh, and eagles are regular on Rathlin off the Antrim coast.

Later that afternoon I walk up onto the side of Slieve Alp overlooking Gleann Cam. The locháns are bright with new rain. The hills and ridges are nondescript folds, like a plain duvet, inviting me to rehearse the names I have learned. Then a squall catches me out in the open and in a few moments my trouser legs are drenched. When it passes, I stay in the same spot, offering the backs of my legs to the bright sun returning. Rain engulfs the scenery for an interval, then, as the squall clears the tops, the falls at Scardaun rise up out of the murk. A loose fleece of cloud pours across the ridge of the mountain.

The bog out here is faintly marked by human intrusion and struggle: a room-sized, six-foot-deep pit lined with tussocks of molinia is all that remains of an old shelter, which was probably roofed with bog oak and loose scraws, the most wretched of all the dwellings of the wretched 19th century, when genteel travellers to the west were dumbfounded by the destitution of the rural population in places like this. When in *King Lear* Shakespeare stripped Poor Tom of almost every comfort of human civilisation and cast him out onto the heath, he might have imagined a dwelling such as this.

On the side of a low ridge near the foot of the hill, a track is scratched out of the peat for barely 200 metres, another mark from those desperate times, to give a pony secure foothold across the rising ground. It leads to a small disused quarry, where for a few years someone took material for building. Stone might have been more readily available in the bed of the river – but was the river out of bounds?

I settle myself with a small ground sheet and my scout blanket to get some rest after the morning's errands and excitement. Nan says that to know the mountain properly you have to sleep out on it; this is my small gesture in that spirit, in the time I have. Cloud and blue sky intermingle overhead when I look up at intervals, then I close my eyes and try to settle an agitated heart with the deep mountain under my spine. I manage this for a while, then the soft patter of another shower arrives, sweeping my face. When it comes on heavier, I pull my waterproof jacket over my head, like a mini tent fly sheet and listen to the raindrops. For a while, there's the feeling of comfort you get in a tent: very close to the elements, and yet protected from them. But here, I eventually have to give way to the fundamentally wet condition of the bog as water trickles against my thigh and shoulder, forcing me to abandon my first trial bivouac out in the open under Corslieve.

The shower thins out and passes, but my blanket is wet, and dampness has crept into my clothes. I am too distracted by my needs to appreciate the vivid arc of a rainbow above Slieve Alp. I retreat in the quiet recognition that 'here is no continuing city… no abiding stay'. An hour's walking (including a reverential retracing of my steps along the quarry track) gets me back to the footbridge on the Owenduff, where my car is parked.

My main reflection throughout this return: is desert a wilderness, or all that is left when man has finished with the land?

The bird was an Irish-bred male sea eagle from a 2016 nest on the Beara Peninsula, Allan Mee tells me. He has also told me about two other sea eagles that have been frequenting the Wild Nephin National Park recently; these are younger birds, but they may already be forming a bond together. I look at the map tracking their movements by satellite: a child's scribble of red and yellow lines through places that are familiar, and not very far from where I live. Now it seems that two young eagles are spending time in the Nephin Beg Mountains, and for the first time in this diary I will have to exercise some discretion as to location when documenting my movements.

21st October

Letterkeen. Storm Brian. Parked at the bothy. Walked up the track into the old Monterey pines.

Bracken is rust-coloured. Green, yellow and orange leaves on the rowan: the deepest, richest red-coloured leaves shaped like spear heads litter the forest floor; a dash of colour on molinia and sphagnum.

Fragments of twigs, heavily festooned with the pale-green lichen of old man's beard, fall onto the track from the tops of the pines. One tuft the size of a fist fell into the river and sank into the stream.

Many large mushrooms under the old pines, rosy brittlegill (*Russula rosea*), with rich magenta caps, turning from convex to concave as they age. Fresh ones are proud and shiny as they push through the grass to emerge.

The river toiled and raged through the narrow gorge, very yellow in its torment: no salmon jumping, it is impossible to imagine them negotiating such a volley of turbulence.

Lots of willow leaves flowing away, small yellow points; willow trees along the river are dots of yellow-green, in a pointilliste style.

Veils of rain were rushing to the south-east in bundles. In the intervals it was possible to walk along the open stretches to reach the shelter of the wood. I stood under one big pine and saw it had its own trickles of water from the catchment of itself.

These big trees kept most of the rain off, but occasionally water would drip down my collar at the back, as if the tree were teasing me, exacting this small price for its protection.

22nd October

Claggan, coastal path. Jessica and I watched for otters at Bellacragher Bay without success. Then we set out along the boardwalk at Claggan. A fine afternoon. The boardwalk has a simplicity and drama, like the runway for a fashion show. We joke that *Vogue* should come to Mayo and put Erris on the map of style. Jessica looked fashionable in her new quilted jacket with the fur-trimmed hood, a single figure against mountains and sky.

We came back along the stony shore. Pine stumps stick out from the shingle; the eroding peat forms buttresses, with little bays of shingle between. The sea was much lower once when this bog was forming. Along the shore, the exposed bank of peat has pine roots at the bottom, just above the glacial till and clay. Pine forest was here once in the early stages of bog formation. You can pick pieces of bark here, several thousand years old, which look virtually new.

A few lumps of a rock on the shore, very like the basaltic tuff I saw in Sicily around Mount Etna. Where has this rock come from?

24th October

Chris and I went to the Blue Lodge today and walked upstream along the river. We saw salmon moving in Keane's, and I saw one fish motionless on the bottom just beside a rock. The day was bright and mild.

We crossed the river just above Keane's pool and set out across the bog along the old track made by the Clives many years ago, An Seanbhóthar. The parallel drainage trench is as clear as it must have been at the start. The track itself is scarcely a seam in the bog at first, then it's a stony surface where the scraws have been scraped aside to expose the base.

We rose one grouse, and then a snipe, which came down again after forty metres. Two of us and the dog ran forward to flush it a second time but we could not find it.

The upper catchment came into view: we took photographs and then came down a steep slope to the river. The map calls this area Bá Bhinn, anglicised as Báfin. A stonechat pair and a meadow pipit beside the river, the first passerines we had seen. A lot of fly life about, including a dragonfly.

We passed many stony runs without seeing any fish, thinking that it may yet be too early for spawning. The water was rather turbid, and there were long filaments of algae wrapped on the rocks like hair. The river was low.

I probed a narrow section of the stream with my stick: five feet deep at least, but we didn't disturb any fish. The first big fish are in Sheep's Head pool, just above the ancient weir. We see nothing at Lurgandarragh either, though the sun is against us and there are ripples on the water.

We have fished the flats many times between here and Cliff pool, but we don't consider them productive. Chris says that he dislikes Cliff pool, as do I, but it should have some good pockets to hold fish. The cliff that gives the pool its name is like an esker, a deep deposit of drift with a lot of sand. By now we are in sight of the Blue Lodge.

We pass the planning notice for a new footbridge across the river. It will make it easier to fish some pools from the far bank.

At Car pool, a sudden big splash, the only one today, from a salmon.

Nothing at Keane's this time as we pass.

A day of elemental brightness: every feature of the mountains perfectly clear on the drive back.

25th October

A white covering of frost on the grass this morning just before sunrise. The first this year. Everything completely still, 'in allen Wipfeln spürest du kaum einen Hauch.'

The eastern sky was a soft pink at first, then an intenser point of pink-orange appeared as the sun rose. It flowed into a clear band of sky under a bar of grey cloud, and then disappeared again into the grey. The cloud shifted to the left, unveiling the sun slowly. Light cast long shadows of trees onto the hoary fields: the air still foggy-soft. Then the cloud moved away, and the sun was a washed-out pale yellowish glare on everything, its angle high enough now to make wet oak leaves glint. It had become the glare of our day, too bright to look at intently.

27th October

As I drove to Kerry and back, the scenery of trees. Maple and beech are the brightest orange and yellow, the ash a weaker yellow. Leylandii cypresses dominate houses and gardens with their gloom. M. agreed to go into the nursing home, but he cried like a little boy, saying that this was the beginning of the end.

Only the usual mildness – and Jessica's unfailing spirit – redeem these gloomy days.

28th October

The hour went back last night. Enter rain, heavy squalls to announce the season. It is not yet cold. The hawthorns have shed their leaves, leaving masses of haws like blood drops on the tips of branches. The first fieldfares are quartering the hedges. This autumn is a match for others in the gloom it brings. We have had two suicides and a death in the locality, and A. is still in hospital three weeks after her accident. Her revival is slow.

Unveiling the Sun

We marched in Castlebar today against the closure of cancer services in Mayo. The main street packed tight with the crowd. Then a squall arrived and the street sprouted umbrellas, like the shields of an ancient army.

29th October

Five whoopers crossed the sky today, calling; bright, laundry-white in a low sun, against the slate-grey sky above the church. Welcome to Ireland.

30th October

Srahduggaun, along An Seanbhóthar. A covering of cloud on the top of Corraun, like a duvet, according to Jessica. The mountain is still in bed asleep. The clocks have been put back.

No otter at Bellacragher Bay.

We walked the Seanbhóthar from the Blue Lodge, with the dog Angel. She flushed three grouse and ran after them, flushed two again, probably from the same covey. Calm. The moor almost completely silent. Jessica makes better progress on the bog, using a stick to probe before she steps. We get to the river over Bá Bhinn in about ninety minutes. Silence and distance. The hillside green above the Bangor trail and Burke's.

We walk back more briskly. John Booth is near the fleece house, checking his cattle. He recognises me from before.

We chat about the fine weather, the season past, what winter brings. According to him, there are twenty grouse along An Seanbhóthar, about half are young birds, half adults.

Some big salmon were caught on the river this year (c. 14lb). He says there's not much poaching now, believes there shouldn't be. The Rock House people have already shot some deer this autumn.

He does not keep a dog because he has a few Limousin cattle, which react badly to dogs and their owners, when they have calves. There were two whiteheads near him. They seemed very confiding. A Friesian also stood, curious, nearby. John petted Angel as we spoke. His cattle were put out in late May and will shortly be put in for the winter. That's five months out. They sometimes travel as far as the junction at Bá Bhinn. He speaks with awe about the winter floods, how they prevent access here.

He showed us where salmon spawn near the gauge at the Blue Lodge.

We parted and took photographs of covered turf ricks on the way out, then went to Ballycroy by the back road, past Sheean Lodge.

It was so warm that we took tea outdoors at the visitors' centre. Jean-Pierre and Nicola are to close tomorrow. Jean-Pierre brought out his laptop and showed us photographs of wildlife from the French Alps, where he spends the winter: golden eagle, capercaillie, black grouse, hazel hen, kestrel. He is well-informed, hunts, takes photographs.

In September or October 2015, he and a hunting companion saw a sea eagle from the road to Bangor just past Tarsaghaun. He said it was 'very square', and is obviously familiar with both species. He knows an area in the Costelloe and Fermoyle Fishery frequented by a sea eagle and described it to us. He talked about wolves returning to France, largely through reintroductions, some of them freelance, unofficial releases.

Everything perfectly calm. We looked for otters again. Saw none. Home by four.

31st October

Hallowe'en. Trees in their autumn beauty:
ash: lemon and lime; chocolate-coloured keys

beech: yellow and coppery orange

sycamore: large husks of yellow

oak: brown and yellow

horse chestnut: deep rust

cherry: had a glorious few days in bloom in spring, then a dull tree all summer: now a deep apricot verging to pink against yellow

willow: green to yellow

alder: just dark green to grey-brown, no yellow or orange, the least dramatic tree

poplar: blackish shards on the lawn, like moulting crow feathers

field maple: yellow

lime: yellow to orange, burnt rust edges

Leaf fall:

small leaves in droves (willow, ash) flaking away in the silence

lime twist and pirouette

maple fall slowly, singly, onto the road, dramatically, like casualties

little breezes push sycamore leaves across drives and tarmac like crabs

If there are no big winds or storms to strip trees violently, they keep their dress of leaves longer; they give way quietly; you can hear the tap and trickle of individual leaves striking foliage and branches as they fall.

*

Afternoon at Nick Harman's in Tully, Louisburgh. Nick believes he saw an eagle flying over his house 'about two years ago,' heading towards Mweelrea. There have been hen harriers on the bog near him but someone 'shot out' the nest, fearing for lambs.

Nick talked about grouse, sheep, lambs, etc.

OCTOBER

The Houstons brought Scottish dogs, sheep and herdsmen to the area in the 19th century. To this day, he believes there's a Scottish strain in dogs and sheep in the area, and a few descendants of the Scottish 'herds'. There's an area south of the Carrowniskey River still called 'the Colony'. His family have been in Louisburgh since c. 1890.

Grouse became very scarce with overgrazing; now there are a few there again. His father used to shoot: grouse were never very abundant; typically, on an afternoon's drive, you might raise three coveys. Unmated cocks would continue to defend territories, excluding others. They would be 'shot out', to allow new birds into territories.

He and his daughter were fishing for trout on a little stream near Uggool 'over ten years ago'. The girl said she saw an eagle.

Nick reports a lot of decline in wildlife generally. Sea trout have all but disappeared from the Bunowen, only a few salmon on his stretch. He also owns fishing rights on 'five to six miles' of the Carrowniskey, but doesn't seem to have fished there recently. The fishery, and hunting rights on 2,000 acres, were things of value on his property, now of little value. (He has about thirty acres of land.)

Pine martens came into his property when Coillte felled the conifer plantation nearby.

Nick believes that small birds have declined generally, as have the curlew. He used to have long-eared owl, not now. He compared their cry to a squeaky gate.

We drank tea in Nick's kitchen while he smoked a cigar. He sometimes comes across as frail or forgetful, but then his features change, lit by a boyish, beaming smile. A new terrier pup nosed about around the table and was occasionally checked from investigating the tabletop.

I show him my eagle map, talked about my eagle research: he is very interested. I give him my phone number. We venture to hope we meet again before too long. It is several years since I was at Tully.

Nick expresses the view that this winter may be severe – an expression of fear, or the idea that a fine autumn must be balanced by a severe winter. As I leave, I say, 'I hope you are wrong about the winter.'

1st November

Weather forecast is for colder weather, with night frosts later in the week and more unsettled weather. Redwing and fieldfare have arrived, in large, skittish flocks.

2nd November

Things I fear this Hallowe'en: big spiders, the prospect of a Trump victory, of war with Russia.

3rd November

Rain overnight, like an old friend whom we haven't seen for months. Part of me wanted a deluge, to see the impact it would have on the Owenduff, but this light drizzle won't bring up the levels.

Winds are due to swing north later this week, with some frost at night, and the forecaster mentioned the possibility of wintry showers on high ground, the first this winter.

Unveiling the Sun

*

Drizzle and mist on the drive to Srahduggaun. Rowan trees without leaves now, lit only by bunches of berries. A hooded crow and magpie in a fight above the road approaching Bellaveeny.

I stop near the hen harrier site at Bellaveeny: a brief clearance, as if the sun were about to break through but then the rain comes in again: the bog that flared briefly in the light, now a dull colour: old heads of knapweed stirring. A stand of birch at the edge of the plantation, heavy with pale green beards of lichen – ghost birch.

Schizostylis (river lily) near a turf rick on the way. I stop on the track 200m from the Blue Lodge. Steady rain in a gentle breeze. The bog spread out to my right is flat, with few features: one sliver of grey water a stone's throw away, the size of a parking space. On the horizon, brown bog rises faintly to two grey ridges and the ground then dissolves into the wet grey. A distant, low line of forestry intrudes from the right. The ridge-line of mountains to the south appears faintly, shifting, then dissolves.

A few old pines around the lodge plead to be saved from rhododendron. Electricity poles and cables converging from the left; more flat bog on my left; the river less than a kilometre away, waiting for this tribute of rain. (One of the last flocks of white-fronted geese in the west frequents this area. On a spring visit with Fergal O'Dowd, we saw goose droppings.)

'When the rain stopped the rain began', James Harpur.

A brighter patch near Claggan Mountain tantalises with the prospect that this might lift.

Wind rises, swaying the car gently with gusts. A small flock of redwing flies across, heading south. I abandon my plans for a walk to Bá Bhinn and decide instead to brave it and go downstream, to see if there are any fish in the big pools, still hoping that I might be rewarded with a pause in the rain.

Fish in Metal Bar pool (sea trout); High Bank; Beach; Fast Run (fish showed at neck); two dippers and ten pipits at Horseshoe. Had lunch sitting beside High Bank pool. No sign of a salmon. V. quiet.

*

The rain kept off (11.00-13.30). I walked the broad shingle stretches along the river, in some places three times as wide as the river. Gorse is establishing on the widest shingle banks, in low hummocks, like arched doormats. They are rooted deep in gravel, on long stringy roots that are impossible to pull out.

Huge chunks of peat have become detached from the riverbank in last winter's floods and lie further downstream, or litter the shingle, as big as black hay bales in some instances. The turf is collapsing along the water's edge as well; grassy sections lie inclined in the water, a few of them as big as pool tables. Small pourings of water spill from the peat banks into the river, with a sound like buckets filling from a tap. Some deposits are sandy rather than rocky, and I feel sure that these were gathered into creels one time to be spread on the land to improve drainage. Entire levels have been raised in this way, and levees built to protect fields from flooding.

A dressing of blackbird feathers on a tussock, with a fox's scat in the middle like a signature.

I examined a lot of deep pockets at low water, trying to remember them for salmon fishing trips, when they would be hidden under big water. I stood for a while at Wall pool where Digby had a fish last May, filmed by a French film crew. A good run there.

At the car, I watched a great black-backed gull flying upstream along the river, patrolling for…?

The last few leaves are blowing off the lime tree at the house.

4th November

Sorting through old notebooks and journals today: 'I can't believe I was ever that bad' (Krapp).

A young eagle from the Donegal project has been roosting at Glennamong recently. The bird spent time there this summer, then disappeared, and has now returned. I drove to Srahmore this afternoon in the hope of seeing it. The NPWS rangers themselves have not seen it yet – its presence is known only from satellite tracking data. While I came upon two ravens enjoying a mid-air romp overhead, it adds greatly to one's sense of the place to think of the possibility of an eagle in 'them thar hills'.

*

Even if the COP26 Climate Change Summit in Glasgow is only a talking shop, as Greta Thunberg and Robert Macfarlane say it is, I'm still reconsidering my driving habits. A hundred-kilometre round trip by car to Ballycroy just to see Corslieve, before I ever start walking, is becoming unsustainable; it's a luxury I can't allow myself every time I want to approach the mountain. As an economy measure, I am going to focus more on the southern approach, via Letterkeen, which I can reach in fewer than twenty kilometres from my house.

The only problem here is that the bulk of Nephin Beg gets in the way; I will have to walk from the south along the Bangor Trail or Western Way past Nephin Beg itself to get a proper view of Corslieve, if I manage that at all in the narrow window of winter days. This provisional resolve (which I am going to have to break, I know) sees Corslieve receding into the distance; at the same time, a different distance opens up, of the intervening kilometres I will have to walk, alone or in company. I think of Hokusai, whose famous views of Mount Fuji are all of a mountain in the far distance, though the sacred peak still draws a whole country towards its magnetic centre; on some of these excursions my sacred mountain might not appear at all.

Nephin Beg isn't the only thing that gets in the way. I spend a large part of the sunny morning waiting for a parcel that doesn't come, and the best of the day is wasted by the time I set out for Newport.

When I pass Lough Furnace I get the first rush of expansiveness, a slightly uneasy feeling of truancy, one that the view of Lough Feeagh, Bengorm and Torc Shléibhe both reflects and validates. The sun crouches low, blazing on the water of the lake, casting the eastern slopes in deep shadow: winter light is here. The ridge overlooking Lough Feeagh deepens from its near appearance in sparkling light to softer, remoter gradations of mist and shadow. The outcrops of Bun 'a Sáil glint in full sun while a fold of shadow runs along the base of Bengorm. An unravelling of low cloud trails whiskery fibres across the ridge of Glendahurk.

At Letterkeen I follow the river through the Scots and Monterey pines to the old gravel pit. Another walker has set out ahead of me with long, rangy strides; I meet a man, then a woman, coming down the track. A couple have pitched their tent beside the river on the other side and are foraging for dead branches to light a fire. This is good to see as late as November. The trail rises above the junction of the two streams at Goulaun and then divides: I follow the right-hand branch of the Western Way, which follows the eastern side of the range.

Much of this landscape is still a havoc of scars and debris from clear-felling, but there are stands of old-growth conifers that have a place in my hopes for this future forest, as nest sites for raptors, including eagles and goshawks, and homes for woodpeckers and pine martens. This is where I saw a young sea eagle some years ago, flying from a perch in these conifers and swinging back towards Letterkeen. With the recent reports from the Nephins, the entire area is pitched to a new possibility

Unveiling the Sun

– of seeing a sea eagle. These huge birds do not show themselves just for the asking, of course; Jessica and I spent a few days on Mull, the Eagle Island, before we saw a pair at close range on the coast. The search for eagles is perfectly aligned to this sentence in Helen Macdonald's book *H is for Hawk*: 'Looking for goshawks is like looking for grace: it comes, but not often, and you don't get to say where or when.'

A hooded crow is calling from another mature grove; I am alert to such sounds now because these crows can indicate the presence of an eagle or large raptor, and in any case there are few other bird sounds at this time of year.

The lichen on the larches under Correen Beg are very beautiful, with a calm beyond science or controversy, and that lone bird is still on Loch Geal, diving and then preening. A tufted duck, perhaps, which my binoculars are not strong enough to see in detail.

After an hour's walking, as I reach the old forestry hut, there's a definite sense of moving away into the wild, just as the managers of Wild Nephin intended. At each turn in the path, a layer of familiarity falls away, as I get closer – to what? I am settling my rucksack in order to sit and write a few notes when the man with the rangy stride appears at the edge of the forest, on his way back.

'Anything about?' I ask in the brisk tone of a birdwatcher. He looks at me doubtfully.

'No, I never see wildlife here, just once I saw a deer near the car park. Just a few birds. I come here a good bit.'

We talk about deer for a while; I tell him about herds here and there, and hunting pressures. When he walks on, I feel that I have the place to myself.

The track goes through an old spruce plantation where many enormous trees are marked for felling, then it emerges under Nephin Beg into a wide valley, slung to the east between

Lettertrask Hill and Cruach Buí. The usual debris of felling is here, but there are also many plastic collars in ranks where broadleaves have been planted to succeed conifers. In other areas, lodgepoles and sitkas were replanted several years ago before the Wild Nephin Project gathered momentum. Just beside these young plantings, some old sitkas like the masts of tall ships stand as memorials to the first phase of state forestry. In addition, there are dense, dark islands of old-growth lodgepoles, a home for hopes and the imagination. The scene has that messy confusion of new wilderness, like Macdonald's Norfolk Brecklands, 'a ramshackle wildness in which people and the land have conspired to strangeness.'

A slim young badger is suddenly there by the track, sniffing among grassy tufts, as oblivious to me as a goldfish in a pond. Then it senses my presence and is off, a quicksilver motion through the mesh of a sheepfence.

I stop where the track turns under Loch na mBarún to brew tea. A movement at the side of my vision becomes a deer in the valley, moving away to join two other hinds among young lodgepoles; it has seen me and turns to make a vigilant stand. A young buck is grazing the hillside under Cruach Buí, the yellow hill. Two more hinds make a ghostly appearance, as muted in colour as the rushes in the hollow, and climb the hillside beside the buck. I spend some time, between mouthfuls of tea, observing the pale rumps of grazing deer among the bold green swathes of pines. I find it comforting to know that these animals have not been spooked on this occasion, and pack up my tea things cautiously. I have scarcely started to retrace my steps when I realise that there are three more deer, a buck and two hinds, close to where I passed a short time ago; but now the buck has seen or smelt me and keeps me pinned by a laser stare. By now some of these deer are out on the open hillside, appearing only as brown flanks, their heads and necks hidden in the molinia as they graze. I would be happy, if I were a painter, to capture them in this attitude of complete ease and concentration, beyond any disturbance.

Twilight softens the outlines of conifers as they recede in failing light. Near the forestry hut, a raven crosses the canopy, calling loudly. Then a whirr of wings, an obscure silhouette deserts the margin of the path, with a movement that is too vigorous and taut for a woodcock: a kestrel it is, performing a few looping glides around the treetops. The couple camped at Goulaun have lit a fire that fills the clearing with a homely smell of wood smoke; their glowing faces, and maybe their hearts, are turned inward to the flames. I pass undetected, camouflaged by river sounds.

5th November

Re-reading *Wuthering Heights*. During her illness, Catherine takes a handful of feathers from the quilt in her bed and sorts them into different species. Is all species identification a form of madness?

6th November

Correen More. As the yellow-orange of deciduous trees fades away with the leaf fall, the browns of dead bracken come to the fore, and the stunted, desolate crowns of hawthorn emerge onto the skyline.

Rowan berries are still abundant, and these bring flocks of redwing and fieldfare to Srahmore, at a time when many species are scarce or absent. Winter thrushes are abundant in the spruce as we approach the Carroll bothy. A small raptor catches our eye alighting in spruce. Jessica and I watch it take off: we believe it to be a merlin from its small size and flickering wing-beat.

I wanted to drive to Altnabrocky, but the foresters keep a barrier locked when they are not here, so we park and set out on foot to walk a lap of forestry track around Correen More. Gloom of green sphagnum on the floor of the forest. We walk for a while against the low glare of the sun, with the urgency of a sheep farmer. Goldcrests in the trees; Jessica remarks on their 'silvery sound'.

As we pass a stack of logs from a recent felling, the perspective continues to open up: much of the area has recently been clear-felled and replanted. The steep side of Torc Shléibhe, with Carraig an Iolair, is in shadow, so the rock is difficult to make out. A footbridge and boardwalk have been built near the track to take the walker onto the bog at Maumaratta – desolate terrain.

The track appears to narrow because pines have seeded naturally and have grown to 5-6-7-8 feet in dense stands along the track; it is as if we are in the corridor of a Christmas tree market.

Coillte have put a section of high deer fence in here, though without careful maintenance it won't be very effective, and at least one breach is visible. I regret not following the deer rut earlier in the autumn and suppose it is too late now. I see no sign of deer on the track. Few sheep here: a Coillte sign warns that stock straying into the forestry will be impounded.

We glimpse a small, dark sparrowhawk dash into a stand of pines: what could it find to hunt in these deserted forests? Small streams are brimming and splashy after last night's rain, pouring into narrow gullies between forestry rows or pouring from peaty banks. A bigger stream (we hear it before we see it) coming from Lough Avoher is a vigorous, swollen flash between tussocks of molinia.

At the three-quarters point, a T-junction takes a pedestrian track to the right: this is our route around the northern end of Correen More. Large rocks have been set in the ground to form wide drainage channels; we use these as stepping stones. The track rises to a pass under the northern shoulder of the hill: wind and rain beat against us as we negotiate the rocky stretch at the Mám; we are careful not to slip on this; our boots serve us well.

A kestrel is hovering above the vehicle track. The third raptor today. Forestry trees are dense and imposing along the last section. There's a pleasing view east, to Mount Eagle and Birreencorragh, with a patchwork of trees and clear-felled areas. Two glittering locháns on the bog. One silvery blade of reflected light is a stream draining water away from the trees; it runs like a lane into a dark recess. Remarkable silence now.

We are wet but content when we reach the car. Our round walk took one and a half hours. Several cars are parked at the O'Carroll bothy as we pass. Lunch at Nevin's.

7th November

The fine, calm weather continues. Severe weather must be getting closer now: as if you are in a dark, silent wood, going deeper, deeper into the territory of a savage animal. Where is it? How long will it be before it shows?

9th November

On the road again this weekend to Kerry. Drove back on Monday through a storm. Was nearly blown off my feet as I stopped at Ardrahan for petrol. I felt some affinity with the old coachmen and wanderers through the winter nights: they walked twenty miles in an evening; we drive 160 miles in the same time – so what? The distances may have changed but the threat of winter hasn't.

This morning the sun bubbled up on the neighbour's field opposite, a great orange flare in the grey, rinsed spaces after heavy showers overnight.

10th November

The lemon and lime of ash leaves is now mostly over; the beech trees are at their best, with burnished copper-orange leaves. A cold, calm morning as mist clears; you can feel winter displacing autumn, though there is no frost yet.

Inversions and fuzzy reflections on the surface of Lough Feeagh. Small flies bring trout and salmon parr to the surface; some of these finger-sized fish show briefly as they pounce at their prey in the air.

There has been rain recently, so the sound of water is everywhere, in the main river and in the throat of small streams and culverts. The deep basins at Letterkeen are thundering like engines, and there's even a seismic stir in the ground from the noise.

The zizzing calls of a scattered flock of long-tailed tits bring life to the riverside. They perch and poise at every angle, like in a painter's study, in the pointillisme of willows. For these moments of their presence, there's a comforting meaning in the cool, wet suspension of the forest.

I stop on the track overlooking the moraine at Goulaun to brew a cup of tea. Clear-felling here a couple of years ago has opened up the vista. Wrens are churring in the wreckage of brash. The river is an open, clarifying, abundant sound, full of the chill that will trigger salmon to breed next month in their dark passion, an impulse that W.B. Yeats understood.

Clouds bring back cold, so I gather up my stuff and move on. For the next hour, with the ease of a level track, I concentrate on the motion of walking, helped along by familiar associations: woodcock alley, view of Loch Geal, old forestry hut, sitka alley, bridge at Srahnawoad, wide clearing, first view of Nephin Beg.

A large, official vehicle is parked at a turning in the track ahead. A jay screeches in the sitkas. Two men dressed like hunters are standing in a higher clearing. As they come down the slope towards their vehicle, I recognise Cameron Clotworthy and Sam Birch from NPWS.

I hail Cameron, who is now in charge of the conservation project in Wild Nephin, and greet Sam, whom I know from a previous outing to watch deer near Letterkeen.

We talk about deer, eagles and an osprey that they saw recently at Goulaun. Deer have become a problem in the north, along the Owenmore River, where up to a hundred have been seen together. Sam mentions forty closer to Altnabrocky, plus a herd of twelve in the valley where we are. We mention other, smaller herds, in the glens between Newport and Mulranny; there are deer on Achill, where they have been involved in a few accidents recently. The guards and the farmers get in touch with the Wildlife Service to voice concern, or anger.

Then our conversation switches to Wild Nephin. There's a new project being developed called the Nephin Forest Restoration Plan, to replace the Wild Nephin Wilderness. 'You've a huge area,' I say. 'I was looking at Barry Dalby's map again lately.' I point towards the north. 'It stretches way up there, and you've another parcel of land, separately.'

Cameron picks up my cue: I'm thinking of the Nature Reserve at Derry, a prime example of blanket bog about six kilometres away.

'We had the ecologists up there the other day. They were very impressed with the habitat. The Derry site is in our area now.'

'We're thinking of flooding some of these areas, let the hydrology do what it's supposed to. And we'll see what we need to do to manage the conifers, but it's not going to be about getting it all back to heath, we'll be managing what's there.' I'm enthusiastic about encouraging the old stands of conifers to grow on.

Then I broach the subject of eagles, while I restrain myself from speaking too excitedly. There are up to four in the area now, they tell me. Sam mentions a sea eagle he has seen, and gestures towards a section of dark, mature plantation.

'It just popped up and over,' he says. My juvenile at Goulaun did the same, flying from the cover of mature trees.

'We might put out a deer carcass,' says Cameron, 'and see if there are takers. Though we did that when there was a golden eagle in the area and it wasn't interested. The carcass just lay there for weeks.'

I give this idea the thumbs up, and show them an image on my phone, from our holiday on Mull, in Scotland, where sea eagles were breeding in an active forestry plantation.

This is all very gratifying, to be at the stage where sea eagles are seen regularly and may even be settling in Wild Nephin. It represents the fulfilment of hopes I have had for many years, since I began to research the history of eagles in Mayo. At the same time, it feels strange to be in the company of hunters and planners, men of almost military bearing, as we talk about the fortunes of these creatures. Wilderness is not something that can simply be left to itself, where creatures can settle into their own dynamic: instead, it involves management and planning, establishing priorities, speaking to stakeholders. I'm even part of the discourse as I tell them that the sea eagle would be a good icon for the National Park, as if I were a marketing strategist. For the moment, though, we are the only people here, as if the ground were being prepared for a nature spectacle that might take twenty years to be ready.

Then I leave them, to head to the Altnabrocky shelter. Almost immediately, there's a different stir in the air, as winds funnelled down from the high ridges of Nephin Beg seethe loudly in the treetops, and full streams from the same slopes add their sound to the growling wind. The track turns right and left under Cruach Buí, then enters the calm of a sheltered stretch where the air is heavy with the smell of pine resin.

Suddenly, among the trees in the gap of the track, the brow of Corslieve appears for a few minutes: innocent, oblivious, intact, and out of reach; then it fades again and disappears, old whaleback of this sea of forest, into its own cold winter element.

Jays are calling again at the Altnabrocky shelter, as I heat my lunch over a small stove. I wonder what they find to eat here. Have they adapted to a diet of conifer seeds?

By the time I get back to Cruach Buí, the official vehicle has left. Four deer are grazing undisturbed on the open slope, two of them quite dark, the others as pale as old rushes. I move along the track, and then look again: they are easy to miss against the tweedy pile of open hillside. When I fix on them a second time, there's a fifth animal, also pale in colour, which has emerged from the rushes of the bottom. The whole landscape is taking its hue from molinia as this plant changes from rich tawny to beige; across extensive spreads of it at low level, the erect seed heads form a distant mist, which softens outlines and spaces. The grazing deer are subsumed within this glow and are anchored here, more subtly, less stridently than the domineering beast in Landseer's Monarch of the Glen. These wild creatures in their stillness are now fitted for entry into myth, or some form of artistic transformation.

Farther along the track, the soft clatter and distinct whirr of a woodcock taking off. A waxing crescent moon over Letterkeen at twilight will become the woodcock moon later in the month, when these birds arrive in numbers from the east.

11th November

Jess and I observed a minute's silence at the Mayo Peace Park in Castlebar. No-one else about. The park still being finished. Two white plastic crosses with poppies, screwed to big ash trees, 'in remembrance'. We decide to do this again next year.

13th November

I mention a November picnic as a way of getting us out, the weather being so mild. A red admiral is feeding on the arbutus at our gate as we leave.

None of the high peaks are visible today, with mist down to about 200 metres. Another couple at Letterkeen are putting on their gear as they prepare to set out; a man in a long, blue waterproof cape returns along the track. One of the sheepmen, who has a key to the gate, drives past with a rattling galvanised trailer.

Jessica thinks that the first part of this walk is the most appealing, and I agree. There is great variety in the mature trees along the river, especially now with extra dashes of autumn colour. As the larch lose their yellow needles, their freight of *Usnea* lichens stands out. There is no recent disturbance from forestry activity, which is only apparent once the view opens up across the clear-felling at Goulaun.

A small raft of tufted duck is sitting on Loch Geal, where that small, solitary duck had been recently. There must be some feeding for them on this lonely bog lake.

We brew tea and eat a sandwich just after the Srahnawoad stream, in a sudden onset of wind:

Breeze God, get up and scatter
The armies of the itchy witch

I quote my poem 'A Midge Charm', though there is no threat of midges today. Once again, the eastern side of Nephin Beg is a place of airy agitation where wind is funnelled by valleys and ridges higher up.

Jessica gets to set the pace and itinerary on today's walk: 'We'll go to where we saw the fox.' Her memories and references are not the same as mine, so it takes me a while to fix on that shaded stretch of track where we once spotted a fox as it entered a plantation. As we come to that curve in the track, a woodcock takes off, flying low across the tree stumps in the valley. Here, between Lettertrask and Cruach Buí is a good spot for deer, I tell her, and she instantly finds a young buck on flat ground in a low, distant molinia mist.

A quarter of an hour farther on, I show her the grassy margin where that young badger was foraging two visits ago. Jessica has a storybook fondness for giving these creatures names, the badger is now called Trevor, and the nearby stream tumbling down the slope under Loch na mBarún becomes Trevor's Brook. We retrace our footsteps from here.

I find fresh otter spraint on a hump of sphagnum beside the Srahnawoad stream. This is today's best find, a sign that salmon are in the pools here, preparing to spawn in a few weeks' time.

We brew another cup at the forestry hut. The farmer clatters past, with six sheep caged in his bright trailer. Then we walk the last hour in mizzling rain. The man in the blue cape is setting out again at dusk, probably to a camp in the forest.

15th November

The evening was damp and foggy, so the supermoon was hidden.

When I got up at 6.15, the moon was hanging over Lavelle's haggard, its light flooding our landing. The house cast a distinct shadow; our cars had moon gleams on their bodywork, and the long monocotyledon blades of New Zealand flax each had a reflected moon at their tip. I took up binoculars to study this moon, which did not excel others I have watched from the house. Instead, it was the trees that caught my attention. A line of bare ash stood against the milky glow of clouds. They were etched black, and wet to emphasise their blackness, in complete lifelessness. They reminded me of D.H. Lawrence's almond trees in Sicily in December, 'Like iron implements twisted, hideous, out of the earth'. Without their leaves, these bare ash were completely objects of winter.

18th November

Travelled to Dugort, to the Red Fox Press. Think Andy Warhol gone to live in a cottage overlooking the Atlantic with an AppleMac and an internet connection. Francis Van Maele, and his beautiful Korean companion, Ham, talked us through their projects, laid out their wares: book collages, screen printing, poetry in translation, blue-fox projects with invited artists. They travel to fine press book fairs all over the world. Francis has been in Dugort for over two years, previously in Foxford; worked in publishing in Luxembourg for many years, after twenty years decided to do something else. A self-directed life. But an operation that involves a lot of travelling to stay afloat. I bought a blue-fox book by Hans Hess.

It rained heavy showers all day. The streams off the mountains in full spate. The moor grass gone to a rich rust, the birch golden, the gorse in bloom: autumnal colours needed a burst of sunlight to ignite them properly, but the sun never materialised. We got cold in the cottage, and wolfed down our lunches greedily at Achill Sound.

20th November

3 am. A declining half-moon. Frosty fog in the valley, giving structure to space, filling the vacant air with moon glow.

Calm, frosty. Yellow-green flakes cascade from the grey willow: they fall silently; leaves from higher up knock off others on their way, multiplying the fall into little cascades. White fleece of sheep give these animals an affinity with frost: they concentrate in the cold, the landscape becomes them. Urgency of tits and sparrows looking for food.

Jessica has put on tights to be warm on our walk. These she has not worn during the last two winters, it was so mild.

We walk the forestry track around Letterkeen Hill anti-clockwise. Breeze against us at the start. Our jaws are numb with cold. Cloud hanging over Birreencorragh and the peaks of the Nephin Beg range. Hailstones from two days ago still in patches, frosting the mountainsides. A small flock of reed buntings in bushes by the track. A patchwork of replanted areas with older stands. Some stands must have been abandoned, where the ground has proved too poor. Larch adds colour in a gully above the river.

The track narrows after two km, where sitka grow tall, encroaching on the thoroughfare. The needles of spruce are bright with the drop glitter of melting frost and a fine addition of cold drizzle from the north. Pleasant spray falling as we pass.

We leave the dense plantation for a more open perspective: Nephin Beg in full view from here, looking quite unthreatening for a climb. Just to the north, a whiter spur emerges, unclear in outline because of low cloud swirling around it: the side of Corslieve, looking mysterious and remote – a kingdom of whiteness, Dáithí Bán's territory. The scree slopes in Coire na gCapall on the side of Nephin Beg are clearly visible.

On our way back, ravens call and mock us from tall trees near the top of Letterkeen Hill. Jessica calls back with a raven's throaty note. Angel and another dog (Daisy) square up to each other as we pass a house. We salute the lady. A very Swabian farm, outhouses neatly whitewashed: a cow's huge head tightly framed by an outhouse window as she looks out.

Animal burrows in sandy banks along the road: we identify rabbit and fox – pale sand printed clearly with a fox's foot.

Fieldfare are still abundant around the rowans at the American monument.

My mind is running on how mountains such as Nephin Beg and Corslieve might be climbed safely in winter. You need to start early and be walking by nine. Compass and waymarkers would be a safeguard if the weather closed in. I plan to drive to Avoher and set out from there.

21st November

I put out a query on Facebook about a cave, which Barry Dalby's Wild Nephin map indicates as being on the side of Coire na nGarú, under Corslieve. This prompts a good conversation among several knowledgeable people about the tradition, but the net result is that no-one has seen this cave, including the late Paddy MacAndrew of Altnabrocky, who was asked about this by Barry Dalby. One of the best climbers in the country, Marzena Rosiak, has also been over this cliff face and found nothing.

All of this confirms my view that there never was a cave on the side of this corrie; instead, the tradition must originate in remote antiquity, based around the existence of an eagle nest site at the same place. This gave rise to the humanised figure of Dáithí Bán, whose whiteness derives from the conspicuous tail of a mature sea eagle; this species was a totemic bird in antiquity, as attested by the bones of Neolithic date found at the Tomb of the Eagles on Orkney. In his human form, the Erris giant still carried traces of his origins as an eagle, with references to stealing from people along the Bangor Trail, and especially to his prowess crossing the islands in Blacksod Bay. The most revealing account of Dáithí Bán's dwelling place was given to Mícheál Mac Énrí of the Folklore Commission by Seán Mac Meanamain (1862-1941) of Tamhnach, near Bangor Erris. According to him, Dáithí Bán's lair at Coire na nGarú was guarded by a strongly fortified entrance. A group of people had used ropes to get down there, but were unable to gain access.

This motif of people being lowered by rope to the dwelling is revealing: it was the way by which cliffmen gained access to eyries and other bird nests, and it occurs in folklore generally as a record of bravery. The association is also reinforced by Mac Meanamain's mention of Dáithí Bán going out to sea for the sake of his health (ar fháirnis a shláinte). Prior to their extermination in the 19th century, sea eagles would have been a regular sight around Blacksod Bay.

22nd November

Walking round Letterkeen Hill with Eleanor and Miguel. The forest is very quiet today, in calm, clear conditions. The ridge of Birreencorragh is a clear line rising to the main peak, the forestry furrows on the side of Leana visible as a pinstripe.

When we come to the far side of Letterkeen Hill, the northern vista opens up: Nephin Beg straight ahead, flanked by Lettertrask Hill to the east: between these two ridges, the bulk of Corslieve is quite distinct, with just a thin gauze of mist. Nephin Beg itself is mostly heather-dark in cloud-shadow, but there are some diagonal scorings of sunlight, and in this proximity of direct light there's a sharpness to the colour of the shadowed mountain.

Corslieve, by contrast, is green-yellow in sunlight, with the rocky faces gleaming in the same illumination. Only Coire na nGarú has a scoop of shadow in its cradle. The eye is arrested by the mountain in the distance and by the hidden promise of the lake in the floor of its great corrie, now just out of view.

The distance to Corslieve today is inhuman, abstract. It is impossible to attach any idea of life or movement to its bulk. Nephin Beg, by contrast, invites exploration: Eleanor asks me about how we might reach Coire na gCapall on the side of Nephin Beg – but today Corslieve doesn't invite any such approach. I tell Eleanor that I have been on its summit a few times, but that sounds like history, a report from another time.

The stillness is more remarkable because it is aligned with a distance of several kilometres, to Corslieve, Glendahurk, and the intervening ridges of Glennamong, Correen More, Lettertrask and Goulaun. The distance is graduated by some of these being lit, or by alterations of light and shadow. The stillness is not that of concealment in mist, say, or darkness, where our perceptions are frustrated; this is a fulfilled stillness, validated by the clearance of a great space where nothing moves, and where the few sounds are isolated noises that can be understood: sheep moan, plane rumble, dog bark. The clear winter light makes us masters of a visible world where Corslieve reigns over silence.

I see fresh deer prints in fine mud on the track, as clear as any I have seen, an exact match for the precision of this day.

A veil of fine drizzle moves across Corslieve and then gradually envelops Nephin Beg; there's a faint rainbow in the eastern sky, but the rain cloud is thin, translucent, and blue sky is visible behind it. This brief smirr is not enough to disturb us: we stop for a snack at the viewing point near Kilroy's. Miguel stays standing; his upbringing asserts itself as he surveys the mountains and forest with eyes schooled in his native Pyrenees.

Lough Feeagh and Clew Bay bright silver against dark islands and promontories in the late afternoon.

23rd November

Perfect clarity after a night's frost. The mountains above Glennamong are brightly lit and a low sun casts black shadows against their flanks, shadows you can rarely see in summer when the sun's light is high by eight. The road along Lough Feeagh is still frosty, in shadow, but the lake is a brightness, reflecting blue sky and a saffron glow of the hillside. A single greenshank is dabbling in shallows by the beach's edge, sending out rings of ripples, centering its world on a small commotion in a corner of a vast mirror.

Pothole puddles are frozen; my car is the first to shatter their ice. On the way in to Lough Avoher I am thrown into confusion by a view of Lough Feeagh from the north, overlooking Letterkeen, and have to check the map to realise that the track to Avoher is longer, that there are more folds of landscape to go, that the road has not yet swung north. Then a white van appears behind me. When we park at Avoher a young man steps out: he tells me he's with others gathering sheep from Nephin Beg today. His dog slips out of the van, and in a moment they have disappeared: by the time I am ready to set out, there is no trace of them.

I turn at the wrecked mountain hut and move up the slope of Cruach Gharbh (410 metres), so-called because of the rocky outcropping on its southern brow. As I move up, I hear crossbills in the plantation near Lough Avoher; then I see a flock of about eighty sheep being driven in a tightly packed stream along the Bangor Trail and turned onto the slope under me. Three more sheepmen emerge from the forest with their dogs: they bring the mountain to life. We move in parallel: I move along the higher slope, they follow a lower line above the Bangor Trail.

A crossbill calls from the plantation; in such bright conditions, with a good crop of seeds, these winter breeders may be getting the idea to nest.

As I move to the top of Cruach Gharbh, the men's voices fade away. A drift of flies punctuates the air and – as if on predator cue – a flock of a dozen meadow pipits crosses the clarity of space with a soft soundtrack of distant water. Mountains are visible all the way to Sligo: Ben Bulben's escarpment rises like a cutting edge at the horizon, and there's even a vague shadow of Donegal's Blue Stacks in a corner. Looking west, the spurs and ridges above Glennamong are clustered against the sun as a gathering of shadows: the best range of mountain cliffs is here, falling sheer off a spur above the valley. My binoculars find the vertical wet rock glistening, a forbidding abstraction above a softer world.

The slope takes me down from the top of Cruach Gharbh towards a saddle between the Cruach and Nephin Beg. The soft vegetation and peat have been eroded away in places, leaving dark hags like islands on rock-strewn ground. The tops of these isolated peat hags, where vegetation clings on and expands slowly, are in places like the foaming crest of breaking waves.

The sheepmen have appeared on the slope of Nephin Beg ahead of me, having come round the base of the Cruach I have just climbed. They pause for a few minutes, and by now must have seen me: an EU or Department of Agriculture inspector whose officious ways might threaten their livelihood? I am in no hurry to catch them up; the warmth of sun on this fine day has me struggling in heavy gear and I keep to my own slow pace. They soon move on and pass out of sight, going round Nephin Beg to the north.

I now have the southern side of Nephin Beg in full view, with Coire na gCapall along its southern flank. A murmuring surface stream gathers water from this side and is visible as a vivid green line cutting through the scree slope. Its softness and sparkle concentrate the eye on an intimacy in the mountain, a first sign to follow, to probe and fasten on.

Now Nephin Beg is topped by a tiny figure – one of the sheepmen has rounded up three sheep on the top and is coming back down. The ground surface up here is still frozen with a patina of ice. This glaze is strong enough on the sheltered sides of the peat hags to give my boots footholds, allowing me to cross. My stick breaks through pink sphagnum resembling raspberry ice-cream; grassy stretches are strewn with clots of hailstones which fell here a few days ago.

Someone on the massif shouts briefly: I scan the whaleback slope but do not see him; he must be on a ridge out of my view. The mountain falls silent again. I check the time (12.30) and decide to make for the summit.

There is a lot of white quartz on the slope for the last half kilometre to the top. I pick up an egg-sized fragment to add to the cairn. The surface quartz, along with the compacted hailstones, suggest to me that white is the essence of this ground. With the white giant, Dáithí Bán, as its figurehead. This makes winter his essential season, when frost and snow gain some purchase on these uplands.

The cairn appears on the skyline: a rough, squarish pillar of dry stone about five feet high with a few blocks of quartz among the grey quartzite. And then, a revelation: there's Corslieve to the north, as if the purpose of this climb had been, not mastery of Nephin Beg, but a humble viewing of the larger, higher mountain.

Now that I am here, it is indeed Corslieve that fills all my attention. In these conditions it is distinguished by a grainy whiteness all across the surface of its ridge, which rises as a gradual ramp towards the distant summit. Dáithí Bán's fort, the summit cairn, is clearly visible over four kilometres away. In stark contrast to this, the low sun produces intense, blackish shadows marking the bowls of its great series of corries on the east-facing side. These are, in approaching order: Coire Leachta, Coire Tirim, Coire na nGarú, and Coire na Binne. The arrangement of these corries in a series along the eastern flank of Corslieve marks their formation by glaciers on the leeward slope, where snow accumulated in the shadow of the mountain out of the sun's melting rays.

The top of each of these zones of blackness encroaches close to the white ridge running to the summit. Nothing in this perspective suggests that three of these corries each holds a lake in its hollow, and that water is glittering within each crucible of shadow.

The summit retreats away into the distance. From this perspective, there's a second, nearer ridge at right angles, stretching west to a shoulder at Tamlesheffaun. This one is like a huge southern rampart defending Corslieve and Dáithí Bán's fort. Because it stretches to the milder, sun-soliciting west, it does not keep snow and hail as long as the main ridge of Corslieve, the white kingdom.

I make a brief sketch of this mountain, sitting beside the cairn. A fly buzzes at my ear. With a few horizontal strokes, I mark the dark peat banks which Fergal and I crossed on our way to the summit, having come there from the saddle at Scardaun. These heights now resemble a northern altar, seemingly inaccessible, lofty and remote.

I go back to Mám Gearr and pick up the stream emerging onto the surface as a small, rocky channel. A brown, medium-sized bird rises and flies; then a second, which I realise is a woodcock. These birds must be feeding in the boggy ground; I suppose they are recent arrivals, not yet settled in the thicker shelter of gorse, bracken and young forestry. A few sheep are grazing near the stream, which has eroded a deep channel into a gravelly glacial deposit. Trees are growing in the shelter of the cutting: a very old rowan with a raven's nest, then a few oaks and poplars farther down. One oak crouches down behind a heathery bluff, reaching its gnarled branches along the rim of the bank, not daring to raise its head any higher into the blast. I take photographs of these trees in their oasis of shelter and think of photography as a gesture of possession, but not as a way of seeing or insight. To be free of the iPad camera; to *look* more closely and see things revealing themselves.

Leaves litter the ground. The stream tumbles across steps, ledges and aprons of bedrock; short cascades pour into deep basins where you could bathe, in another season. I stretch my hands into the clear water and relish the pressure of icy cold like a clamp; I rinse my face in the meltwater and move on, refreshed.

The Bangor Trail crosses a spur to the north as a thin seam in the ground. The valley floor is lit by silver coils of the Baunduff River. I sit by one of the oaks as a low sun touches the mountainside to the west. These dark spurs and ridges offer little to the eye, with the glare of sun over them.

The track I rejoin is a mess of sheep marks and bootprints where flocks and their herdsmen have just passed. I follow in the wake of their traffic for the last two kilometres and then turn at Avoher to get back to the car.

Lough Avoher is largely frozen; a few mallard are dabbling at the western end.

I watch the flock of gathered sheep approaching Letterkeen on the far side of the plantation. The mountains are now almost completely devoid of stock, except for a few waifs and strays. As I look east, only Birreencorragh is showing any white, like a silverback gorilla leaning forward on all fours. The hilltops are still radiant, with the forestry hollows now in shadow.

There's a pastel-yellow overlay on the western sky as the sun sets, a blush of mauve in the east. Thus endeth a beautiful winter's day.

25th November

Lough Furnace. I sit in the glare of a low sun, as a squall rocks the car gently. The storm has not quite done with us yet – in fact, there is never a conclusion. You clean up after snow, or a storm, thinking, 'That's over now, we've had our measure of bad weather for a while', then another nasty gale brews up before the wreckage of the earlier one has been dealt with. Our minds, and with them our hearts, can't ever get the measure of the weather. Weather is something wild, in the early modern sense, a threat to our safety, forever louring in the chaos of nature, ready to pounce.

Glendahurk. A flock of redpolls were feeding intently on birch seeds. They settled long enough for me to get a proper look. These birds are normally very skittish and restless, but this time, there they were, brightly lit in an interval between showers.

I reached up to a low branch and picked one of the tiny brown lanterns of seed: it crumbled between my fingers; the seeds that these redpolls were after appeared in the powdery chaff, little glinting fragments, like mica.

I did not need to weep
at Glendahurk
when the showers did it for me.

27th November

Today I had to clear out the store because we've been listening to rodents overhead for a few nights. There have also been odd squeals from the corner of the garden that I thought were rabbits being caught by a stoat, but now I figure they may be rats. Everything got swept out to deprive them of food. One little mouse ended up in the ash bucket and jumped up and down several times before finally making it to the rim; then he jumped off and ran away to the end of the garden. Our house gradually acquires a history among the animals, some of them unwelcome. I am pleased about the bats in the tower.

Eleanor has sent me photos of the mountains around Lough Feeagh with their first winter covering of snow.

28th November

Coire an Earraigh. With the neighbour's border collie, Angel. The bad section of track at Avoher is now very bad: the car barely made it and I won't attempt that again.

I walked directly from Avoher to Coire an Earraigh Mountain. A stretch of wet, plashy bog before the ground rises. Grouse droppings in three places, two of them fresh. (I have also seen droppings in Glennamong, but they are generally very scarce in this part of the range.) As the ground rises, I take bearings from the ridges nearby: Cruach na gCaora and Cruach Gharbh.

Today I am minded simply to climb and get there, keeping my head down, remembering what happened to Lot's wife, but of course my resolve weakens, and I turn round to survey Nephin Beg and Corslieve. They have lost last week's white powder of hail. From this angle, the summit of Corslieve presents its snake's head shape. Shafts of light appear on the Mullet and Gweesalia to the north-west, and a few gleams are spread across Tamlesheffaun.

The high, narrow hump of Corr na Binne (716 metres) rises to my left, like a threatening monster. It has never looked like this before. A raven, one of a pair, rises above the ridge and does his sideways flight-dive. These birds are truly at home here, never more so than in winter.

At about 450 metres, I get my first view of the crags of Coire an Earraigh, a few modest outcrops with a tenantry of sheep. The last elevation is a stroll across a tight sward onto a ridge forming the summit at 628 metres. The cairn is not often added to; I place a small offering of quartz on a shoulder of the topmost stone.

The two lakes of Coire Dá Loch are below me, with breezes skidding across their surface. Although the wind is severe, jaw-freezing, I venture on to get a view of Coire Hob, a corrie in the northern corner of Glennamong, and inspect its cliffs for an eyrie site – but they are too low. I am tempted forward for another ten minutes to get a better view of Coire Dá Loch, then the wind defeats me, and I decide to turn around. I skirt the main summit of Coire an Earraigh to get back to my approach route.

Angel sniffs places in the ground where other animals have been. At one point, she rolls on the heather and rubs her back in the vegetation: when she stands up I see a recent, grey fox turd. A little deposit of fresh hashish-coloured droppings – probably a hare's – also detains her.

I cross to a bog lochán I had missed on the way up. About ten metres by fifteen, it has five butts of peat heavily overgrown with sphagnum and heather, and is completely undisturbed. Each little island is doubled with an inverted reflection on completely calm water, like an underside of coral on a sea reef. Small flies move about the surface with a vibrating action of legs which causes tiny waves. We cause more ripples as we walk around the margins of the pool.

When we drop down towards the stream, a woodcock rises silently from wet grass and treats me to a good view of its dark markings. The stream off Cruach na gCaora tumbles and splashes across levels of bedrock before slowing down and forming a series of meandering loops with grassy margins. This stream will soon become the Bawnduff, a tributary of the Owenduff, which enters Blacksod Bay at Srahnamanragh. The noise of these short cascades diminishes in volume as I stride back towards Avoher.

Out on the flat bog, an old sheep's pelt with a skull and a few bones where a carcass was picked clean many weeks ago. Many pieces of old Scots pine also obtrude through peat, the skeletons of an ancient forest.

A group of sheepmen and their dogs are on the track near Christmas tree alley: they look startled by the approach of a vehicle from the top. I stop to ask one of them for the name of the peak I have just climbed. Coir' an Earraigh he calls it. Maumer Dougher means nothing to him. Again, a name for a hollow or valley next to a peak gets transposed and is applied to the peak itself.

29th November

The forestry gate at Letterkeen is open, and an NPWS jeep passes, on its way up. I shelter in the bothy while a shower clears. The air, clouded with fine droplets, is full of water murmurs. This time I go the edge of the river among the pines, pottering along. The bracken leaves have all but collapsed into limp rusty cloths, but the stems still stand up stiffly, scored orange onto the scene. Big hanks of molinia adorn the riverbank on the far side. Mushrooms are disintegrating like melting ice, a few glistening orange caps still lighting the mossy floor. The root plates and trunks of fallen trees are becoming nurseries for ferns, seedling spruce and hemlock, rhododendron, and smaller flowers. Whereas deep moss monopolises the ground, these harder, emergent surfaces of woody bark and roots provide nurseries for other plants. This shows again why you should not tidy up the forest floor, but allow timber to rot away and add to the complex relationships of the forest. The spruce and hemlock seedlings rooting on fallen logs become part of a cycle of regeneration.

   The water runs fresh and strong in the main river and in the Goulaun stream; I search the pools for salmon but can't see any, though it is still a couple of weeks early for spawning activity.

   The Nephin Forest feels like a true rainforest today. Gusts of wind shake heavy jewels of water from the branches. The forest floor is a deep carpet of soft moss, which thrives here because of the conditions of constant saturation and mild temperatures in winter. As mosses have no roots, they need a constant supply of moisture to photosynthesise; their sexual reproduction is also entirely dependent on water. Mosses are the first primitive land plants that evolved sexual reproduction: while aquatic algae could rely on water to transport male sperm to female eggs, mosses needed a film of water in their terrestrial habitat to get the male sperm cells to the female egg. Even with constant inundation and humidity, the chances of the sperm reaching the egg are, according to Robin Wall Kimmerer, 'vanishingly small'; on the other hand, mosses propagate easily from detached fragments, which effectively clone the parent plants, 'without the costs and inefficiency of sex.'

The moss growth throughout the forest is much the same as the process that leads to peat accumulation on the bogs, which makes me wonder about the health of its trees. The big Monterey pines, potential sea eagle nest sites, are not regenerating. Planted here for ornamental, scenic reasons in the 1800s, they feel like museum trees, though their deeply fissured boles are a haven for insects, and I am puzzled not to have seen a treecreeper here yet.

The lodgepole pines are another story. Up to very recently, lodgepole was planted here on peaty soil as the staple tree crop, but in many places it has not taken well and has been abandoned by the foresters as not worth harvesting. At times it grows as a bonsai tree only a few metres high after several decades and acquires a character totally at variance with its original role. In other situations it forms ghostly, skeletal groves where light penetrates, allowing mosses and molinia to thrive. There's so much of this across the Nephins that it amounts to a new habitat type; the trees themselves are in decline, with many of them dying, shedding bark in broad sections like shin guards, and disintegrating from a threadbare crown. And yet, there are variations to this pattern: on one hillside the lodgepoles are ailing, while on an adjacent slope with different ground conditions the trees have a dark, dense character; these are not commercial forestry trees, but ones which are slowly reclaiming their native American aspect.

A bright interval takes me across the Goulaun stream, onto the top of the moraine that I have viewed so often from the Western Way, but rain comes on, forcing me to stand tóin le gaoth in the hope that it might pass. The ground along the river is heavily marked by sheep, and in today's conditions my mood turns melancholy – why, I wonder, did God design animals such as sheep that could be turned out onto these waste places and survive? If it were not for sheep, we could contemplate the desolation of the winter bog in its primordial state; instead, the bog in winter becomes a scene of official neglect and general indifference. These gloomy thoughts are only partly dispelled by a hastily consumed bag of crisps, eaten standing up.

I abandon the trek across the top of the moraine and return to the river. The stream that runs down from Lettertrask to join the Goulaun stream is a delightful, buoyant celebration, running wide and shallow at this point. Still in mourning for loss, I think of the numbers of salmon that must have run here in 'the old days', under the patrolling eyes of ospreys and sea eagles.

There's a fine grove of conifers on the srah between these two conjoining streams: some old Monterey pines with lodgepole and sitka. Most of the lodgepoles are ailing, but occasionally a favoured tree gets enough room to prosper. I enter the grove and have to step across fallen logs as I proceed. All that remains of some trees is a crumbling, yellowish column of pulp, encased in a shell of old bark. I notice some bore holes and wonder whether there might be food here for a prospecting woodpecker, so I try some pecking myself with the point of my stick. I jab at fragments of bark and they come away easily. A centipede runs off; then, in a mouldering fragment, I find a dormant woodlouse and a couple of millipedes, curled up in a winter dream. Meagre fare indeed, but it might be enough to sustain the first great spotted woodpeckers when they reach this forest, as must happen very soon.

The Monterey pines, the oldest trees in this grove, are eminent specimens forming a high canopy overhead. Still with a sense of absence, this wood is waiting for a large raptor to touch the cold maze of trunks and branches and bring it to life.

A recent gale has brought down many fragments of these trees, with their heavy freight of lichens. I photograph a single tuft of *Ramalina* lichen on the ground, a windfall star.

30th November

Last night there was a funeral at the church. The first we knew of it was a line of car headlights approaching from Clogher, forming a starry necklace that extended across the darkness of our big window. At its head was the lit box of the hearse.

December

1st December

Foggy days. Yesterday I drove to town through a maze of lace curtains, with blue sky somewhere overhead. Patches of fog were dense, whereas at other moments the gables of houses appeared on nearby hillsides, lit by a bright sun. Town was damp-cold, reduced to a blurry grey-scale of wet tarmac, blackish trees and bare lampposts. A woman with a camera was capturing this novelty on Bridge Street.

By four o'clock it was all over, fog had closed in again, removing any distant perspective. Small sounds were amplified in the dimness; the world was reduced.

After nightfall there's a double darkness in fog. Deprived of lines of vision, our eyes and spirits turn inward: we rely on memory, we resort to the habits and modes of our relationships. If these are not happy, then this time of year can be especially testing.

Fog and darkness facilitate stealth and concealment. Angel

was struck by a car at our gate two evenings ago, but we were unaware until Margaret arrived at the door yesterday morning. The crimes of Victorian London were committed at night in the dark warren of a foggy, smoggy city, and the dense air guards the secret of 'whodunnit'. The hound of the Baskervilles roamed a similar territory of winter fogs in Devon. The London my parents knew in the 1950s was a city of pea-soupers, of smogs so thick you could lose your companion if they strayed more than a few metres away from you. My father told a story of having lingered one evening at the house of a friend and of having to set out on foot to get home, of getting lost for hours in the smoky murk of unfamiliar streets. 'There was soot in your handkerchief if you blew your nose.' Dublin in the 1980s was similarly afflicted.

These stationary, high-pressure fogs are unfamiliar here. Atlantic breezes usually clear them away from the coastal west. We have sat for days at Jessica's family's house in Worcestershire in thick fogs while Wales and the west enjoyed winter brightness and blue skies.

3rd December

Lough Feeagh. I park beside a newly renovated house at the edge of the track and set out. In the partially cloudy morning stillness, the colours and textures of the bog are especially vivid, although there's not a single flower left. Here the predominant tones are chestnut and mahogany, there the greens and raspberry reds of sphagnum, elsewhere the bleached peroxide of mat grass. The latter is a tenacious plant with densely matted roots going down into the peat. Some denuded areas are pale with this plant. Black bog rush must be a favourite with sheep, because many clusters have been cropped to a spiky mat. Deer grass is dark brown, with bunches of stems hanging like a horse's mane. Cross-leaved heath is now a greyish spike with faded papery flower heads.

On the slope above me, a group of faint grey smudges take shape as rowan trees in a loose group under an escarpment.

The waters of Lough Feeagh break on black rocks along the margin. When I saunter down to the water's edge, I find a low causeway running into the lake for about ten metres, marking what must have been an old boundary. A greenshank flies up from the next stretch, the living spirit of this black-and-white shore, calling in the grey light.

By now, there's morning light over Glennamong: layers of soft-lit cloud on blue-grey; Torc Shléibhe is a warm buff colour guarding the entrance to the glen, which is still a shadowy backwater, its deep green plantation giving nothing to the morning, reflecting nothing.

A soft whirr rises from the margin: a little jack snipe, returning silently to a band of rushes twenty metres away, having done enough to inhabit this silted shore with its intriguing scarcity. Rocks and mud are streaked with its droppings.

At the northern end, the lake forms a sandy bay where the Glennamong River makes a few deep, slow turns before losing itself in the lake. Large chunks of peat, which river floods have coaxed away from the banks, are scattered on sandy deposits. I walk the sand, inspecting fresh bird and animal tracks, and occasional little scrapes where a fox probed the ground. My own bootprints are spread around within a few minutes, among signs of fox, snipe and greenshank.

The last kilometre of this lakeshore walk takes me along the slow bends of the river until I get to shallower water where I cross. A raven and two lesser black-backs are turning lazily in an updraught off the south-east shoulder of Torc Shléibhe.

My walk takes me round the top of the lake, along a forestry track and on to a tarred road at Srahmore. I'm soon heading south, past the small Catholic church, where woodland nestles close to the road. Oaks and willows are releasing a thin cascade of dry leaves; they make tapping, sifting noises as they fall; the lighter, more buoyant oak leaves scrape and tumble on the stony road surface. Leaf-fall is the main sound, with the chatter and peep of fieldfare and redwing fleeing away.

From this vantage point, the mountain ridges to the west, above Glennamong, are clustered in a forbidding sequence: Maumahieran off Bengorm, Corr na Binne and then Coscéim above Glendahurk. The arête of Coscéim, which I staggered across several years ago, is sharply defined in this light. The slope of Torc Shléibhe is thrown across the whole sequence as a diagonal rising to the right.

The little bay beside the jetty echoes with calls of greenshanks, shrill peals across thin water. I know that their underparts are as bright as quartz, but here it is the pencil black of their wings and upperparts that brings the black lakeshore to life, like its incarnation: stone made feather and flesh.

I stop near the promontory fort to check the map: eight km done, with five to go, by my estimate. There's an impatience in me now to get back to the car, which I can see on the far side of the lake. From here I resolve to concentrate on the motion of walking by ignoring things close to me, little disturbances and features on either side of the road. In this way, I think, distance will pass and I will be back at the car without much effort. But then another realisation is added to this resolve, when I look around me and notice how the landscape can shift as I walk through it: a distant promontory that I have been watching for two hours has now drifted behind me; the little bay ahead that surprised and challenged me with its curved recess is now under my right elbow as the road rises away from the shore.

Walking is a gradual tilting of perspectives; with the parallax of ridges and summits, your feet can move mountains. As I walk on, the loop of my trail encloses the lake and makes it mine provisionally, within the boundaries of the day. And so, with these recognitions I make more progress, even if I still fail to concentrate only on the motion of my feet on the road surface; the awareness of distance, of mountains and promontories shifting behind me, is still part of a desire to get on, to walk the kilometres and to arrive. Although it has helped to pass some time, and the space that time accomplishes, this noting of progress is still haunted by my impatience to finish.

It is only later, having passed the Marine Institute on Lough Furnace, within a kilometre and a half of the car, that I conquer this impatience and its waymarking attentions. As I climb a short slope through hazel woodland, fatigue itself tempers my impatience, depriving it of the energy it needs to agitate. At the same time, there is no anxiety in me any more about the finish, because the finish is near. I am becalmed in two ways, by fatigue and the confidence that I am soon to arrive. There were instants along that stretch of road between the hazel wood and the fish counter when I was completely suspended within the action of walking, as much aware of distance covered as of distance still to travel.

And yet, in the memory of the day, that spell of immersion in walking, of pure concentration, is embroidered with objects and recognitions that must have interrupted it: some flowers of herb robert on a sheltered wall in the hazel wood, the hazel catkins themselves, fully formed and ready for extension in a couple of months, plum-coloured buds on hawthorn, and small agitations on lake water that might be of fish.

When I get to the lake outflow at the fish counter and look over the bridge, I notice the wake of a salmon as it moves about in shallow water over the gravel of a redd. It is well camouflaged but for a white mark near its dorsal fin which allows me to follow it. Then it dashes off into deeper water with a brisk riffle of fins.

I meet my neighbour Dominic Conway driving a quad bike

with fencing in a trailer. He points to a nearby house as his home place. I discover that my neighbour in Fahy is a sheep farmer in the Nephins. We chat for a while, sharing an unstated change in our views of each other.

Four greenshank and two snipe, one a jack. A collared dove in song near the Marine Institute. Gorse and Mediterranean heath in flower.

There are some posh houses near Lough Furnace. Their owners must work in the city. The houses are empty, the dream deferred.

5th December

With Jessica at Letterkeen. Clear and calm, scarcely a ripple on Lough Feeagh. At the bothy car park, we meet a Scottish painter with his easel, on his way to the Letterkeen Loop to do some sketching.

We go out along the Western Way as far as the Srahnawood stream where the bridge is being rebuilt. A tiny dead pygmy shrew beside the stream, scarcely a foot from the dark fox scat that Ged and I had examined. Big bristles along his conical snout. Raptor chatter from above the trees. I see a sparrowhawk fly across the clearing, agitated by these intruders into its territory. We haven't seen a kestrel here for weeks, so this hawk is a precious gift.

A lone hind is visible on the ridge of Correen More on our return, presumably from the herd of a dozen or so that is established on the other side. I fancy it has come up to the top to survey the territory to the east. It stands there for a few minutes until it finally registers our presence and bounds away. However many times you are told about excessive numbers of red deer in the hills and forests, seeing these creatures is always a thrill.

The mosses in the shaded part of the forest and on the big rocks at the basins are very beautiful. I look at them through the x10 hand lens: some are like braided glass, gleaming with moisture; others are miniature zucca palms just a couple of millimetres wide, or like fronds of miniscule ferns. Another very intense, deep-green moss on a capsized tree stump looks like the invasive heath star moss, *Campylopus introflexus*. I have as yet few names for these wonders; instead, I pick up some fragments of lichen on old larch twigs and rehearse three generae: *Usnea*, *Ramalina*, *Cladonia*.

My back is very tight today and Jessica takes the rucksack for most of the walk. I tell her that this ailment must be from looking up at the sky for eagles. When I meet God in the next life I'd like Her to tell me how many times an eagle has crossed the sky behind me as I was looking away.

A big, round, fluffy cloud like an Afro hairstyle on top of Birreencorragh.

6th December

Towers of cumulus on a blue background, with sliding drifts of grey cloud, as storm Barra approaches. Elvira, Colin Guilfoyle and I walk the new riverside loop at Letterkeen, discussing approaches to the Nephin Forest restoration plan. Colin is a zoologist by training, with a keen interest in bird life; he is now embarking on a Ph.D. on the habitats in this area. I repeat my message about the value of old-growth conifers, the interest of a new 'Second Chance' wilderness, the dynamic of a habitat that is allowed to develop, and talk about the diversity of the forest: crossbills, siskins, coal tits, redpolls, reed buntings, jays; then the warblers: sedge warbler, willow warbler, blackcap, chiffchaff, grasshopper warbler. Our conversation continues on topics dear to the heart of any ornithologist in this area: merlins, hen harriers, eagles, and ospreys.

We pass the exclosure planted with Scots pine seedlings from the Burren, where a native population has recently been discovered. Elsewhere in this area, there's an extensive ground layer of rhododendron scrub, with old-growth lodgepole. In some of these stands, a few trees continue to grow handsomely while the rest ail and die. This leads to a question in my mind: if the ground conditions are the same, why should some trees prosper while others decline? Have these trees formed mycorrhizal networks that respond to poor soil conditions, and decided that only a few individuals have the resources to thrive? Biochemical signals in root networks allow trees to respond in this way, as if they made communal decisions to defend their populations.

For the first time, I hear about plans to remove plantation from a large area in the north of the forest, around the lakes at Altnabrocky and Tubbrid, to restore bog habitat, as at Derry.

Elvira tells us about trout and salmon in the rivers, and reckons that the weeks before and after Christmas are the best for salmon spawning, though I tell her that I have not yet seen any on the redds. Salmon run all the way into Lough Bunaveelagh, she says, where there is also a population of arctic char.

After our walk, Colin and I take a drive, clockwise, around Letterkeen Hill and meet a sheep farmer who emerges from the forest, returning to his tractor parked on the track. After a few exchanges, he offers this piece of wisdom: 'Every day you go out onto the mountain you see something.' This adage from a sheep farmer is excellent corroboration of something I have often thought, and is also a good guide for a student starting out on a programme of field study. Colin's early work will involve identifying transects and study areas, but part of the experience will be the unexpected nature of some findings.

'The great spotted woodpecker will be here soon,' I predict.

'Nature is always changing; some things are leaving, others are arriving.'

7th December

Aleš searched Coire na nGarú on Sunday, in excellent conditions, climbing the left-hand ridge, for signs of a cave. Found none.

8th December

Storm Barra. Walking from Newport to Eleanor and Miguel's at Treanbeg. Jays calling in the old wood. Wind pushing white scuffles of surf off the surface of Lough Furnace. Very violent turns and surges in the far bay. Molinia leaves caught on the mesh of sheep wire freaking out, like a wild exclamation.

Large blocks of sandstone conglomerate steadier than ever in the gale, while the thin pelt of grass stirs and shivers. White breakers in a great host from the north advancing across Lough Feeagh. There was snow overnight, but it is spread as a thin peppering on the higher slopes, except for Nephin itself, where white cover is continuous on the top of the cone.

Unless they are revealed in the pure whiteness of fresh snow when the wind drops, mountains are unremarkable during a storm: blurred by a filmy agitation of mist and showers, they withdraw from our view into their own epoch. We are tense with attention to our own needs and are careful with our feet. Things assert themselves for brief intervals: haws like baubles on a bare, twisted tree; a holly shaken by a force that might sweep the tree towards you. Old sitka spruces, planted singly or in lines, are noisiest of all. Wind seethes and hisses through millions of needles, twigs, branches and lichen; the tree absorbs the storm around it, converting it to sound. As I walk past, I think one spruce is about to topple, but it stays put where it has been for seventy years.

The road drops down among hollies and hawthorns as I approach Eleanor and Miguel's house. A tractor passes, with a black bale of silage hitched to the rear. The driver is hunched, intent, deep-jawed, a Ted Hughes double.

9th December

Glennamong, with Eleanor and Miguel. We parked before the bridge and walked into the glen. Conditions were exceptionally bright and calm. A large flock of reed buntings – what are they feeding on?

Afterwards, as we sat with coffee and snacks near the car, a small dark falcon crossed the valley, flying low over the ground, and perched on a boulder at the foot of Torc Shléibhe. It was as if the ghost of Emily Brontë had visited, still abroad on the western moors. Ten minutes later, as we packed up to leave, the bird was still there, enjoying the last afternoon light, its breast turned towards us.

The light is never more intense than at this time of year, the shadows never deeper.

10th December

I cleared oak brash from the garden in the afternoon and added it to dry hedging under the alders. Some of the oaks have shed all their leaves and are naked and proud, showing off this year's growth; others still keep a rich dress of dry, brown leaves. Narcissus buds under the alders are showing now, about 1 cm high. When I had finished I sat in the lounge and watched a gibbous moon intensifying in a darkening sky.

*

John Montague's death was announced today.

Unveiling the Sun

I climbed to its source once,
A journey perilous, through
The lifeless, lichened thorn
Of MacCrystal's Glen, a thread
Of water still leading me on
Past stale bog-cuttings, grey
Shapes slumped in rusty bracken,
Littered with fir's white bone.
'The Source'

*

Jessica showed me a bird-shape silhouette on the wall by the door: its shadow was from low sunlight reflected off a car. As passing cloud made the sun unsteady, the shadow pulsed like a living spirit.

The calm of this mild weather amounts almost to complacency. Where, I wonder, are the storms, frosts and snowfalls? Will this exceptional weather be clouded by met office statistics announcing records broken, vindicating the progress of global warming?

We look up, and around. We can see things because we are not beaten and hunched up against pelting rain. The commercial conspiracy of Christmas winds up its tawdry music box and exhorts us to buy goodness. Goodness is all around, and it's free.

The patter of rain against the window as I write – a novelty.

11th December

This morning's clear sky allowed sun into the house at a low angle, the midwinter light falling on walls that see little direct sun during the longer days. A gleam of light on the leaf litter under the oaks on our half acre.

The Srahrevagh stream much lower than the boiling flood I saw last Friday. On my way up the track, the waterfall at the Lep was audible. I crossed the fence about half-way up and scrambled through the plantation, going towards the river. Out into a clearance, some old wood from an earlier felling rotting away, soft, crumbling, with crops of lichen, including devil's matchsticks. Willow and birch, plus a few older firs pushed over by storms.

Coillte planted broadleaves here, in compact stands on the srah, cradled by the stream's meandering. Mostly oak and birch. The birch stands have a silvery, parchment-coloured bark to illuminate, with their bright pillars, a December day with low light. They seem to gather an intensity to themselves. As I rounded one of these copses, the soft, heavy whirr of a woodcock taking off (I did not see it). They feed along grassy margins of the track where cow pats attract worms and other invertebrates, leaving a pin-cushion pattern of their probing bills. A few stands are flooded now, given all the heavy rain there has been lately.

Some willows are heavily decorated with pale lichens, like fluffy clumps of starburst. An old tree near the culvert at the top (where the stream flows under the track) has partly recumbent trunks, a milky way of these fluffy *Usnea* and *Parmotrema perlatum* [powdered ruffle lichen] suspended over the stream, and a dark plating of bryophytes on the trunk.

I stepped over a few old cultivation ridges as I crossed a partly wooded srah. Human history is sparse here, but the story of the new bothy holds enough to capture the heart: four people were found at the McCann house (now rebuilt as the Glen Augh* bothy); they had died of starvation. This was reported to Michael Chambers by a man in his nineties, who had it from his grandfather. I ate my lunch of avocado pear, apple, and dried fig as a guilty luxury, sitting in the door of the bothy.

*Glen Augh, Gleann na nEachú, glen of the horses

13th December

Upper track, Glen Augh. Very quiet in the forest; goldcrest and coal tit. Light drizzle at first, then a clearance, still mostly overcast, a patch of blue sky to tantalise. The track, which had been opened up by heavy machinery and fresh fill, has greened over within a year, a heartening result after the devastation, though there were no signs of pine marten.

Today the eye is drawn to the mosses and lichens along the track and draping the trees: *Thuidium*, *Entodon*, *Rhytidiadelphus* – moss generae.

A cock pheasant in a boggy field at Srahmore – goshawk food.

15th December

Watching *Patience*, a film about Max Sebald, on the internet. Sebald's account of his walking tour of Suffolk, *The Rings of Saturn*, has a wide resonance among English readers, writers, editors and photographers interviewed for the film. Seen through the lens of Sebald's keen erudition, the East Anglia landscape is richly layered with histories – of invasion, erosion, abandonment, dereliction. The Suffolk coast is a theatre of decomposition, of land crumbling away, of structures being left to the sea, or to dissolution by weather. The quaternary touches on history in the shadowy legacy of Dogger, that territory sunk under the North Sea.

Among the commentators there's a feeling throughout that English landscapes are now tiring under a weight or palimpsest of associations, and, concomitantly, that the genre of landscape writing has itself peaked in England. One writer complains gently that going for a trek was an easy way of getting a story:

you go out for a few hours and then write 700-1000 words about the experience. (This is exactly the technique adopted by this diary.) Another says that the over-use of topography actually erodes all sense of place, to the extent that *place* becomes *space*, where we are free to deploy almost anything. *Place* should ground us, tie us to specifics of experience; *space* is free and open, like an empty room in a gallery. In Sebald, a vast drift of beached herrings can connect to a photograph of dead Holocaust victims; a painted-over emblem on a train leads him to Imperial China. Joyce's *Ulysses* teaches something similar about the power of the associative imagination taking its cues from a particular place: Stephen on Sandymount Strand.

Rob Macfarlane makes a distinction in his narrative between British and European romantic writers treating nature as a place of *recovery*, from the burdens of city, work, and society, and American romantic writers responding to nature as a place of *discovery*. Where does this journal fit?

13:00-15:00 Letterkeen. I am surprised by the streams gushing white and full – when was this rain? Cloud a blanket cast over bog and lake, turning the woods under Eleanor's place into a narrower arena of winter hues: wine-dark canopy of a birch wood beside rocky terrain where wheatears will return in about three months' time.

The Srahmore and Goulaun streams are magnificent, though I don't see any spawning fish. This festivity of fresh water needs to fine down before we can see salmon. Mizzle turns heavier under the raining trees. My jeans are drenched by the time I get back to the car.

The forest floor is festooned with lichen on fallen twigs from high in the trees, a pale manna of *Usnea* and *Ramalina* like soft snowflakes littering the ground. Some larger branches also, wrapped in a thick swaddle of pale growth.

Unveiling the Sun

16th December

Last night we heard a barn owl calling close to the house. Yesterday there was a full moon: although the evening was overcast, when I went out at ten to close the gate, there was a luminous quality to everything.

17th December

Fantastic sunrise and sunset. Salmon-pink skies. We were at Séamas Mac Philib's funeral. He was buried in Aughaval cemetery, with the Reek and Clew Bay behind him.

18th December

Srahrevagh. A driech morning, low cloud slow to clear. I park at the pull-in beside butterfly alley. The sound of streams running high. Where the soft drapery of cloud does lift away from the ridges, the outline of horizon is clear, precise: dark-brown hill on a backdrop of grey, with a glow of western sunlight not far away, but not yet showing. Once I park the car and turn off the engine, there's a nervy moment when, all noise and driver's reactions suddenly absent, my attention settles at a different level. The open window admits sounds and the seep of cold. The object of my journey is suddenly here – I have arrived in this coveted place – but as soon as I am confronted with the accidents of the elements, of weather, vegetation and sound, my desires stall; they are called forward out of the complacency of their settled preferences, and confronted with more raw material; another day, maybe a new encounter to deny or challenge the security of private imaginations. When I hear the call of a jay from the plantation mix of birch, lodgepole, and rhododendron, the place has given me an echo of my intentions, so it is time to pull on the boots and set out.

I take photographs as I go: reindeer moss, devil's matchstick, and red sphagnum in the shade of western hemlock. A small party of reed buntings and a bullfinch pair.

I turn at the Upper Track: this section is very quiet, the silence broken once by a calling raven overhead. The stitchwork of a woodcock's bill in a cow pat. A few goldcrest calls. I fix a goldcrest in the binoculars and the intense yellow recalls the yellow of a salmon fly, a line to unlock the day.

When the track emerges to open ground on the left, I pause, and sit for a while. There's life at the forest edge: a robin, coal tits, goldcrests; a little fly drifts in the air overhead. Sounds of wind and water farther down in Glen Augh are rising towards me. No vehicles have been here in recent days; another little gang of coal tits forages through the branches as I write. Then the calls of goldfinches, their charm crossing the grey backdrop.

When the track turns left (avoiding the firebreak taking you out above Jamesie's Well), it enters dense sitka forest, making me think of Friedrich's French cavalryman looking at the German *Urwald*. (I am writing now in this deadzone, where I stopped for a sandwich.) Still no signs of deer – just a dead pygmy shrew on the track with its side eaten, some kind of token, a pledge of something I have not yet worked out. The spruce are impressive, some good timber here.

The track turns towards Eidir Gleann, the glen between, and comes to an end. I scramble up onto the open ground among stunted, but still very beautiful old lodgepole pines with neon green needles and black bark. They grow here in open groves, as if planted decoratively. Here, and at the top of the glen, reaching towards the ridge at Leana. Not for the first time, you sense an impulse to create a natural-looking forest, even where the exercise was meant to be purely one of tree husbandry. A decorative, picturesque need took over.

On this ground, with a noisy stream cutting through the deep glen, there's a slight dizziness in the big perspective that has just opened up: the flank of Birreencorragh overhead, dissolving into cloud.

It's raining again as I go back, having noticed a plunge pool that might serve on another occasion.

A gunshot, then, after an interval, another. The only sign of deer life today comes as the noise of death. They don't show on the track and must keep to the forest, not to give the hunter a clear line of fire.

The roadside streams are full; little cascades fall from the peaty banks. The bigger streams make a full-throated plunging noise as they enter and issue from culverts running under the track. At the top of the roadside bank, water pours from a heavy, green fleece of sphagnum moss. The ground is saturated, and the excess makes a happy abundance of water everywhere, fringing the road, and forming longer streams in the little glens, feeding the Glendavoolagh catchment of the Deel River.

The sun has set by now. I stop to listen. It's still too early for a singing thrush, even though the evening is calm and mild. Blackbirds are firing off volleys as they go to their roosts. Here and there a robin tries a few riffs of song, and a wren makes extraordinary noise in the undergrowth. It must be woodcock hour.

I get to the car and drive off: the first cock is there in the headlights an instant later, seeming as pale as a greenshank, before it hoists itself into flight from the grassy margin. A second flushes from the middle of the track, and just after Frankie Mac's, another one hunkers down at the side of the road and does not take off. Bats hunting along the margins of the rhododendron near Srahmore Lodge complete the day. A new quarter moon is a blur behind thin cloud. Very mild.

19th December

Jess and I sweep out the Letterkeen bothy in preparation for my birthday lunch tomorrow.

20th December

My birthday. Jess and I have invited Chris and Lynda, Yvonne, Ged, Eleanor and Miguel for lunch at the bothy.

We serve smoked salmon for starters: the fish was caught on the Owenduff by Michael Kingdon and smoked by Chris. Veg. curry is the main course.

The day is cloud-foggy and cold, but there's an awareness that the sun is shining on the higher tops, as it was yesterday, when walkers on Buckoogh could see Birreencorragh and Corslieve above the fog.

After food, it's time to get moving, and everyone elects to go upstream towards Goulaun to look for spawning salmon. Water levels are low, but the streams still run bright and clear across the redds; paler stones shows zones of disturbance where fish have been excavating.

Chris reports a salmon in a pool above the meeting of the waters, which I saw yesterday just a hundred yards downstream: this fish had a distinctive white mark on its back.

A few surges in a long, narrow pool – I spot a salmon of about 5lb; a second fish with stippled marks on its back looks like a sea trout. These are very scarce on this catchment because of fish farming in Newport Bay. Seeing one in a spawning pool is a wonder, but can a fish like this find a mate?

The forest is extremely quiet. A robin under the trees near the concrete bridge. A grey wagtail near the bothy contradicts my assumption that they desert these upland streams in winter.

We are almost at the solstice. Eating and sitting out today has been a hardship, but people are eager to mark the solstice and the turn of the year. All our plans have been put into doubt by the spread of the omicron variant of Covid and our expectations have tapered off, like the light. There's a tacit hope that better things are in store next year with the return of the light; deprived of wider distractions, we are turning to primary rituals of food, company, and trust in the living world.

As all the gifts and Facebook wishes arrive today, I find I have a surplus of good feeling, and would like to share it out with people whose lives are in any way blighted by anxiety, cruelty, or neglect. For me, the returning light represents hope. The planet that nurtures all of us should bring comfort to those who are in any way shut out from care.

21st December

The sun was visible just after sunrise this morning, flaring out of a cluster of spruce trees. There were strips of Georgian blue within gilt-edged clouds, all that glare and light veiled in the nearer distance by a hailshower. The hailstones shot onto the grass, becoming visible as they rebounded briefly. The length of the day is less remarkable than the low trajectory of the sun, flooding the house with light at unaccustomed angles.

The house is shaken by pelting squalls of hailstones; when they clear, warm shafts of sunlight penetrate the rooms.

22nd December

Grey squalls of rain sweep across the mountains. As we approach Lough Feeagh, Glennamong is in bright light, with a deep shadow in the bowl of Coire Hob; Buckoogh is a shadow within a shadow. As the rain passes, light comes up from behind us, and the dark heather is vivid against the grey distance.

The rust colour of bracken is also intense on the promontory: this is now surrounded by blackish agitated water, with white-crested waves. The lake surface is an unusual shiny blackness, like a steel coil, beside bracken and yellow splashes of flowering gorse.

The far side of the lake is dark brown: deer sedge lower down, with heather on the higher ridges – all of it now veiled again with a passing shower of rain.

We park near the sheep yard and walk through the forest towards the bothy. Wind hisses and hums in the tops of the conifers. Deeply fissured trunks of Monterey pines are like pillars in a classical temple; I walk among them in awe. A sunburst lights the wet bark and the trees shine. Small streams in the drains are full, forming ale-coloured pools with bubbling froth; a heavy swell pouring over the weir.

We shelter from rain for a few minutes near the gravel pit. More pines have fallen into the river from erosion and lie along a surging pool full of the kind of gravel that looks ideal for salmon redds. Salmon are crowded in the spawning stream at Cong right now, but none are here. Jessica observes that we never see the heron on this river.

Wind gusts strongly along the track, rising from the gravel pit and snatching thin, papery wisps of molinia into the air, which fly past us.

Sunlight is strong, when it appears, as we go back. A cloud comes across the sun, creating neat sunbeams in a fan-like cluster spreading from behind the cloud. There's such an intensity of light it produces burn-out on the lake surface, the promontories near us are reduced to black fingers holding out in the giddying dazzle.

23rd December

Jess and I walk at Glen Augh, Srahrevagh. We follow the upper track at Glen Augh all the way to the firebreak and drop down to Jamesie's Well. Jess is unsure at first, does not enjoy the enclosed section of the track overgrown with spruce and rhodo. Virtually no bird life to report, either seen or heard.

The 700-metre section of the firebreak takes us half an hour to negotiate; the slope is very wet, sphagnum-soft.

Mount Eagle and Gogín are just visible, though Leana and Birreen stay overcast. I'm disappointed about this, because Nephin Beg is clear.

The streams converging at the little booley hut beside Jamesie's Well are a delight. The biggest comes down to the hut, tumbling steeply in a series of cascading steps and brief pools. A stand of larches along the bank is heavily laden with *Usnea*: Jess says we're 'walking in a winter wonderland.'

Elvira tells me that the trout in this stream were all flushed downstream by a huge flood in July 2009. We follow the stream and then step through a narrow strip of old-growth plantation to get to the track. We then cross an obstacle course of fallen trunks, with draperies of moss, ferns and heather on the vertical root plates, the growth out of sheep reach. Wind-throw like this creates barriers to sheep: I would let this all go, to grow and collapse.

We return to the car and drive to the bothy, where we fry bacon and brew tea. A sheepman arrives, unloads about thirty blackfaces, and drives them out to the river; he sends them downstream, then corrals them with his two dogs, and coaxes them into crossing the stream to the Maumaratta side.

The day is calm and mild, much milder than my birthday. The bacon cooks, the water boils on stoves set on the table outside. Another December picnic.

There were two crossbills flying over at the edge of the old plantation in Glen Augh. Goldcrest, wren, dunnock, raven. Jessica saw a sparrowhawk fly along the river below Jamesie's Well.

24th December

We had seen many holly trees with berries in November. I wanted some berry sprays, drove to Lough Feeagh in rain, the brooks full. Sheep grazing along the road. I walked down the track to the Brontë house, many trees stripped; one tree in a narrow ride, surrounded by birch, was numinous with berry clusters; I took my secateurs and cut a gabháil of branches.

Isolated trees had been stripped. Thrushes feed in the open, where they can watch the approach of the sparrowhawk, but in the narrow, enclosed space of the overgrown track, the sparrowhawk has the advantage of surprise and agility, so the thrushes are shy, wary of this place – and the berries on that tree were untouched.

Abundance of holly berries where the sparrowhawk rules.

Holly berries in rain –
Not a thrush in the lane
Of the hunting hawk.

25th December

Altachuiny. The wind singing. Hopkins's 'Inversnaid'. Breezy overnight, making the roof slates rattle. Rain sets in as I get to Lough Feeagh. The first stream near the youth hostel is running high: it cascades over the rocks in white turbulence, without a pause for rest. One short pool near the road gives the water a reprieve for a moment, where it clears to the colour of champagne and then plunges again into a white effervescence. The rocks forming a narrow channel are very dark, highlighting the white water.

Wind is working hard on the lake. It tries to throw the lake onto land, but the waves cannot stir the concrete pier from its foundations. It manages only to fling some spray over the wall of the jetty, where it dies in a pleasant splash.

Out in the centre of the lake, wind scours the surface, occasionally forcing white scuds of spray into the air, pushing them across the water until they disperse.

Small streams on the flank of Torc Shléibhe are now foaming cataracts, brilliant white lines against the dull background.

I park at the bothy and walk downriver at first, then turn right where the Altachuiny River joins the Holes River, and I am on the Bangor Trail. The Altachuiny River is in full spate, draining the flank of hills forming the northern rim of Glennamong. It runs clean and clear around large greyish boulders. Truculent gusts of wind are hitting me full on as I step among the stones of the trail: the doses of oxygen are too much at first, and my heart flutters a few times as my body adjusts to the air and exertion. Still, the day is very mild and I don't need gloves.

I cross one footbridge, a galvanised steel structure that has already yielded somewhat to the winds. The river has eroded through a moraine deposit, leaving a high bank to the left where a few deciduous trees find refuge. Some way farther on, a stile leads into the forestry, back to a solid track. I decide to push on for about a kilometre to the second footbridge.

The ground is more open here, with young lodgepole pine to the right, and hillside to the left. Deer sedge is abundant, giving the terrain a reddish-brown appearance, but the ground is much degraded from overgrazing. Stones that were set down to reinforce the trail have now emerged in relief like the backbone of a famished animal: like narrow stepping stones, they require care as you step across.

The hill in front is Cruach na gCaora, and gives its name to the stream I am headed for. I walk on stony ground: one section is a four-metre wide avenue where an inch of water is running as a glistening sheet among potato-sized stones: I am walking on water.

The Cruach na gCaora stream crosses the Bangor Trail in a modest cutting with a few refugee trees. There's a single holly tree in the shelter of the embankment just downstream from the footbridge. I pause here to take in this ancient relic. The trunk emerges horizontally from the glacial drift, its brown, wrinkled skin like the neck of a large herbivorous dinosaur. There are tiny magenta clusters of flower buds ready to open in the nodes of its sprays. On the windward side, many of the branches have died and are bleached, but even they defend new, vigorous growth, especially on the leeward. This great plant must be centuries old.

When I step over a fence into the forestry, the vegetation changes and I find I am grateful to Coillte for providing a sanctuary for plants in this valley. Molinia and ling heather are thriving along the banks of the stream, the former with great pale swaying bunches of stalks, like uncooked strands of spaghetti. A few six-year-old pines were cut recently, probably as Christmas trees, but were discarded and lie here beside the freshly cut stumps.

I follow the stream on my way to the track; there are little animal runs in the grass, which look like those of an otter: but what would keep an otter here, near a small, barren stream? I am answered by another slow, deep channel joining from the left: there's enough here to keep trout and eels, the otter's favourite.

The stream has now become a river eroding a ten-foot clay bank topped with a three-foot section of peat. There's a lot of fresh debris on the bank itself; other detached sections of turf litter the shingle on the opposite side. There are even two dead trees still attached to their peaty turf, detached from the high ground at the top. A rusty line meanders across the section of grey clay – the famous iron pan – like a red river seen from space.

Unveiling the Sun

I continue through tall lances of molinia, among stars of sphagnum, and bless the forestry as I do. A simple stile gets me over the fence to the track.

Rain comes on intermittently as I walk the kilometres to the junction at the forestry gate, which is now closed. A little group of goldcrests makes small noises in the trees: they flit about, tiny fragments of life in silhouette. As I rejoin the Holes River, the track is littered with pieces of larch and the shaggy growth of *Usnea*, debris from storm Barbara. One forlorn sheep calls from the forestry and runs away up the track, apparently disorientated: its companions are calling nearby, but it has not heard them and is running away, like a distressed creature that may not survive.

The Carroll bothy serves me well today: I change out of my heavy gear and put on light shoes.

*

As I step back into the house, a sudden commotion flings redwing into the air, and then a tiny falcon – a merlin – shoots past, moving to the left. These lowland fields are much more frequented now than the deserted forests and hills, so the merlin has to leave his moorland stronghold to hunt here. Kestrels seem to have deserted the Letterkeen forest, as have redwing and fieldfare.

26th December

A window in the weather. Calm first thing, with partial brightness, an anaemic sun shrouded by thin cloud. We make sandwiches and go.

At Lough Feeagh, a fox disturbed from the roadside bolts away among the stones of a bluff, holding his tail high – no, we are not the hunt with him as our target.

A flock of curlew rises from the lake edge and circles about.

They are silent, so I can't distinguish them from whimbrel, but at this time of year they must be curlew, not the May bird.

Jessica exclaims 'Deer!' as we climb the track up the Srahrevagh Valley: two on one side of the road, three to the right. They have seen us, and have moved away, but the right-hand trio want to rejoin the others and eventually cross the track and enter the cover of rhodo and pine. This must be a regular crossing point from the Srahrevagh Valley towards Letterkeen Hill, where I have previously seen deer prints, but never the animals until now. I congratulate Jessica, she brings me luck with deer sightings just as my friend Chris Huxley brings me luck with otter sightings.

We drive the upper track and park, giving ourselves a mile or so of track to walk to the start of Eidir Gleann. The forest is very quiet as ever. A vehicle, approaching from behind, must have seen us, because the driver turns round again and retraces his tracks. Park ranger? Hunter? We don't know, but I am pleased to think that we might have frustrated someone's deer hunt this morning.

Once we leave the track, we follow the hollow of the glen just above the stream. A woodcock flies off from its daytime form in heathery growth, a dash of white droppings marking its fright as it leaves. I think later: another prey species for my goshawk of the future. Then, on the horizon, a small sparrowhawk appears briefly in pursuit of a pipit. It leaves again, the only raptor we will see all day. I scan the sky for eagles.

This lower section of the glen is heavy going: heathery, mossy tussocks, with old drains cut by foresters in the early stages of the programme, and never used. These cuts have filled with sphagnum and now have to be negotiated to avoid a muddy immersion up to the knee. Marks of sheep are not pronounced here, so the ground is soft, and mosses and lichens luxuriate.

All the trees in this valley are spruce, forming some dense

stands lower down. The stands become more scattered higher up, in a way that resembles the natural appearance of trees at the top of a tree line. It is hard to know if these smaller, dispersed trees were planted in the early stages of afforestation or if they grew naturally from seed dispersing from established trees farther down. In either case, they give this valley a 'natural', scenic appearance. There are magnificent tussocks of moss growing among these spruce trees. Here, as elsewhere, the winter forest is almost completely silent.

After some careful footwork across very wet bog, we climb through a break in the trees to reach the ridge forming the rim of the valley, and continue the walk to the top of Leana. We have come to the tree line, but the ground is still scored by long, parallel drainage ditches filled with vivid green sphagnum. I imagine teams of local men – with what kinds of vehicles and equipment? – doing this work for their valued wages while at the same time shaking their heads at the enterprising planners who believed that trees could ever prosper in such a high, exposed location. Sure enough, the wind picks up, and, as if to demonstrate a principle, I come across a few small spruce trees growing in a peaty trench, hunkered down, out of the wind.

I am struggling on the last, hard yards. A decayed fence line, which marks the limit of the National Park, tempts me towards the horizon. I walk past the fragmented wooden remains and continue for another hundred metres across tawny moss. There is no cairn at the top of Leana, though there is one farther down at the summit of Gogín (Mount Eagle). I plant my hazel stick in the ground and wrap my saffron snood around it, as an improvised flag. The summit of Birreen has been swallowed by cloud, only its stony flanks are still showing. The glen below me, Díogan, is a dizzying drop to the varicose loops of the Deel River on the start of its journey through Glendavoolagh towards Lough Conn.

Jessica will surely make it now, I think, as I retrace my steps, leaving the marker behind. I whoop with exultation and come back past the old timber post and flop down into a hollow where I unpack refreshments. Jessica comes past me, and continues to the top. She returns, holding my stick and snood, as I thought she would.

After a snack and a drink, with the summit behind us, there's a welcome easing of pressure. The way down is gentler, helped by the flow of gravity and the assurance that we have time to spare. We walk towards the beginnings of a stream flowing through its own small valley at the head of the main glen. Coming down the hillside, we enter a dispersed grove of spruce trees, between five and eight feet high, with a browse line at about three feet; under this line, the trees have the dense structure of a hedge, like something created by topiary.

Jessica: 'Good King Wenceslas looked out on the Feast of Stephen, / Where the bog lay round about, deep and soft and uneven.'

In the first of these browsed trees, a robin calls, and flies into the dense interior. Such a resilient creature in this loneliest of places.

As we enter the stream's cutting, the noise of running water is welcome; we hear a river being born, making its first whimpers and chuckles out of the saturated obscurity of moss and peat. A wren calls, pottering on a rock by the water, another hardy pioneer of upland spaces, perhaps surviving here only because of the extraordinary mildness of the winter. A second wren, a little farther on, will complete the tally for today.

Eidir Gleann is a remarkable place, one which it is difficult for our perceptions to accommodate. An upland valley completely dominated by spruce trees (lodgepole pine appears only at the very end, as you approach the resumption of the forest track), all of them relatively young, in woodland history terms. There is no rhododendron, willow, or any other scrub. The ground is scarred by drainage cuts, many of them unused. In some respects, this forest is a deadzone, but its appearance, with many trees scattered in an apparently natural arrangement, makes it almost picturesque. A picturesque scene, though, that is the outcome of an abandoned experiment in tree husbandry. There are no old boundary walls or huts, no field systems, nothing to imply earlier settlement, and a scant placenames heritage. The stream enters a narrow gorge at one point, where you would like to send a competent bryologist to explore the plant antiquity of the area. Otherwise, the silence of Eidir Gleann echoes to the ghostly noises of the people who worked here in the 1940s and 1950s, and whose legacy is now guaranteed in these silent forms. There is no fallen timber yet, no lichen colonising broken stumps of trees pushed over by storms, but that will come in time, given that most trees look healthy, even though the ground is saturated.

Woodland is something we normally infuse with nostalgia, with a richness we project either from a general past, or a past embroidered with our own memories. Eidir Gleann defies this because its time is now and in the future: the ideas of abundance, variety and accommodation all lie in its future: for now we have to be content with the calls of a few small birds, a drift of flies, and a half-dozen trespassing sheep that flee into the cover of the trees, as if fearing hunters.

I finally drop down to follow the stream and get a photograph of a plunge pool, which I'll reserve for later – a dream of summer adventures.

27th December

BBC TV programme on moss:

Moss remains from a British Antarctic Survey core revived and grew again: the stratum was dated at 1,500 years old.

Moss grows extensively on volcanic landscapes in Iceland, the first plant to do so, forming a soil layer for flowering plants to colonise.

Japanese gardens venerate moss, and exclude other plant material; science, gardening and zen, all in one. The programme opened to show a gardener sweeping maple leaves from a mossy floor under trees.

28th December

Lough Feeagh, western shore. Parked at 11.30. A calm, cold day after frost in the night. The lake very calm: a sheepman on the far side calling to his dog. Ravens calling at the crag, Bun 'a Sáil, where the slope starts up the ridge to Bengorm.

I went through the gate and turned down towards the lake. Close to the water: the scattered bones and fleece of a sheep that had been picked clean months ago. This kept the ravens, foxes and hoodies fed for a while.

A little farther along, a stream comes down to the lake in a small gully; old hawthorns and a couple of hollies spread on the slope close to the lake; some fieldfares feeding here. One holly heavily cropped with berries, a very old tree with two used hoodie nests. A mess of feathers plastered to a rock under this tree where a hawk had plucked a bird it had killed. Another holly nearby had no berries, but a hoodie nest with remains of a rabbit on the rim. Another tree along the shore, an ancient oak. Then a stonechat – what can it find to eat?

A fish shuffled away from rocky shallows under a shoreside tree. Three teal and two mallard moving away from the margin. A great black-backed gull pair calling as they fly over. A few gorse bushes partly in flower; sheep have bitten off shoots in their quest for food – they must be very hungry.

The shore is very dark and inert. Virtually no birds on the

lake, as usual. A lace-margin of ice has formed, like a Libeskind design, all angles and sharp triangles, an inch proud of the water. An ancient stone jetty. No snipe or greenshank, just the same three teal and mallard pair. The thin crust of ice at the margin has deterred the waders.

I approached the bay with the delta of the Glennamong River – a skein of mallard rose, calling. A couple of teal. One cormorant. The ridges above Glennamong lightly dusted with snow. I stopped for a snack and decided to turn back for home, staying higher, not following the shore.

The bog is very wet and degraded here: deer sedge, mat grass, and black bog rush, with thin remnants of cross-leaved heath and calluna. I took photos of deer sedge, textured like the heavy hair of a pony's mane, and mat grass. Black bog rush was a deep green, with pale, faded fringes. A thin patina of ice, which my steps crunched over.

In a fenced-off field near the track, the vegetation is very different: deep tussocks of molinia in a miniature woodland of bog myrtle. A reed bunting pair.

On the higher crags above the car, heather in profusion, and scattered rowan trees.

31st December

Walked to Brockagh, did the new loop behind 'the manor'. Beeches wonderful in their muscular main trunk and branches. The manor was lit very brightly as we walked back; louring grey sky to the west as a squall approached. Rain came on as we went down the drive to Anna's. She was not there.

We got fairly wet walking home, but there was an exhilaration in the exposure, the air dancing bright, adorning the shorn hedgetops with rain glitter. It is we who let it down, with our muddy traces.

DECEMBER

We drove into Westport after lunch: intensest glare on the wet road surface from a low sun. I saw this glare on Lough Feeagh last winter, as if water gathered winter brightness from the dormant earth.

A near full moon in the evening.

NOTES

Introduction
Robert Macfarlane, *The Old Ways* (London: Hamish Hamilton, 2012)
———, *Landmarks* (London: Hamish Hamilton, 2015)
'The thing to be known': Nan Shepherd, *The Living Mountain* [1977] (Edinburgh: Canongate, 2011), p. 108
'The darkened river': Sidney Spencer, *Newly from the Sea* (London: H. F. and G. Witherby, 1969), p. 115
'it comes, but not often': Helen Macdonald, *H is for Hawk* (London: Jonathan Cape, 2014), p. 5

1st January
'Once an eagle rock': Jim Crumley, *The Eagle's Way* (Glasgow: Saraband, 2014), p. 57

10th January
Seton Gordon, *The Golden Eagle* (London: Collins, 1955)

14th January
'like a guilty thing surprised': William Wordsworth, 'Intimations Ode'
'thinnest boat': Percy Shelley, *Prometheus Unbound*, Act IV, line 206

27th January
'sheepwrecked': George Monbiot, *Feral* (London: Allen Lane, 2013), Chapter 9

10th February
'Peregrine O'Cleary': the English name of Cú Choigcríche Ó Cléirigh (fl. 1630-62), one of the four masters whose Annals were compiled in Donegal between 1632 and 1636

1st March
'in his thin sarcophagus of ice': J.A. Baker, *The Peregrine* [1967], introduction by Robert Macfarlane (London: Harper Collins, 2005), p. 129

NOTES

4th March
'The Great Eagle/ An tIolrach Mór': Micheál and Tomás Ó Máille, *Amhráin Chlainne Gael* [1905], new edition by William Mahon (Indreabhán: Cló Iar-Chonnachta, 1991), pp. 68-70 and 175-76
'Féilim Mac Dhúill': see Tim Robinson, *Connemara: A Little Gaelic Kingdom* (Dublin: Penguin Ireland, 2011), pp. 353-55

13th March
'Nuair a bhíonn sneachta ar Néifinn bíonn sé fuar in Éirinn': 'When there is snow on Nephin it is cold in Ireland'

14th May
'which knew neither seasons nor gardens': Samuel Beckett, *Molloy* [1955], edited by Shane Weller (London: Faber, 2009), p. 48
'But the eye, let's leave him his eye': Samuel Beckett, *The Beckett Trilogy* [1959] (London: Picador, 1979), pp. 330-31

25th May
'literally frightening': Mark Wormald, *The Catch: Fishing for Ted Hughes* (London: Bloomsbury Circus, 2022), p. 52
'Barrie was electrified': ibid., p. 50
'the whole purpose is': Ted Hughes, 'Learning to Think', in *Poetry in the Making* (London: Faber, 1967), p. 61
'strangers': see poem of this title in Ted Hughes, *River*, with photographs by Peter Keen (London: Faber, 1983), p. 60

19th June
Roger Deakin, *Notes from Walnut Tree Farm* (London: Hamish Hamilton, 2008)

17th July
'R116': the call sign of an Irish Coast Guard helicopter that crashed on Blackrock island, north of Achill, on 14th March 2017, killing all four crew members

18th July
'The darkened river': Spencer, *Newly from the Sea*, p. 115
'The sound of a river': ibid., p. 136
'August Evening', in Hughes, *River*, pp. 92-94

Unveiling the Sun

11th September
'hummadruz': a word usually applied to a persistent buzzing noise heard in the open, with no apparent source. I use it here to refer to the sound of the landscape, in this case caused by wind. At other times, through the silence of the Mayo landscape, you hear a faint noise made by water running off the hillsides in countless trickles and streams.

12th September
Barry Dalby, *Wild Nephin* (Enniscorthy: EastWest Mapping, 2015)

24th September
'Place and a mind': *The Living Mountain*, p. 8
'It is worth ascending': ibid., p. 19
'Simply to look': ibid., p. 102
'The thing to be known': ibid., p. 108

13th October
'You meet yourself on the moors': Elizabeth-Jane Burnett, *Twelve Words for Moss* (London: Allen Lane, 2023), p. 38
'topographies of self': Macfarlane, *The Old Ways*, p. 26
'not only means': ibid., p. 24

20th October
'here is no continuing city': T.S. Eliot, *Murder in the Cathedral* (London: Faber, 1935), p. 18

25th October
'in allen Wipfeln spürest du kaum einen Hauch': 'in all the treetops there's scarcely a breath', from Goethe's poem 'Wandrers Nachtlied', 'The Wanderer's Night Song'

3rd November
'When the rain stopped': 'Roscommon Rain' in James Harpur, *The Dark Age* (London: Anvil, 2007), p. 11

4th November
'a ramshackle wildness': Macdonald, *H is for Hawk*, p. 7

NOTES

10th November
'a previous outing': 'An Early Start', *Irish Pages*, 11(1), pp. 62-64

21st November
'The most revealing account': Mícheál Mac Énrí, 'Seanchas ó Iorrus', *Béaloideas* 13, 1943, pp. 173-237 (p. 205)
'ar fhairnis a shláinte': 'for the sake of his health'

23rd November
'It is worth ascending': *The Living Mountain*, p. 19

29th November
'vanishingly small': Robin Wall Kimmerer, *Gathering Moss* (Corvallis: Oregon State University Press), p. 25
'without the costs': ibid., p. 27
'tóin le gaoth': 'backside to the wind'

10th December
'I climbed to its source': from John Montague, *The Rough Field* [1976] in *New Collected Poems* (Loughcrew: The Gallery Press, 2012), p. 65

24th December
'gabháil': an armful, the amount of hay, turf, etc., that can be held within outstretched arms

27th December
'BBC TV programme': *The Magical World of Moss* (Zadig Productions, 2023)

Unveiling the Sun

The maps contain Irish Public Sector Data from Tailte Éireann, the Environmental Protection Agency and the National Parks and Wildlife Service, licensed under a Creative Commons Attribution 4.0 International (CC BY 4.0) licence. Map data for roads and forest cover was obtained from OpenStreetMap (openstreetmap.org/copyright). Elevation data was obtained from Open Topography (Hengl, Tomislav, Leal Parente, Leandro, Krizan, Josip, and Bonannella, Carmelo. 2022. Continental Europe Digital Terrain Model. https://doi.org/10.5069/G99021ZF).

For your own observations

Unveiling the Sun

Unveiling the Sun

Unveiling the Sun